Signs, Symbols & Ornaments

Signs, Symbols & Ornaments

RENÉ SMEETS

VNR **VAN NOSTRAND REINHOLD COMPANY**
New York Cincinnati Toronto London Melbourne

First published in paperback in 1982
English translation copyright © 1975 by Van Nostrand Reinhold
Company
Dutch edition copyright © 1973 by Uitgeverij Cantecleer bv. de Bilt
under the title *Ornament, Symbool, & Teken*
Library of Congress Catalog Card Number 75-2823
ISBN 0-442-27800-4

Printed in the United States of America
Photographs by Ton Smeets unless otherwise credited

Van Nostrand Reinhold Company
135 West 50th Street, New York, NY 10020

Van Nostrand Reinhold Ltd.
1410 Birchmount Road, Scarborough, Ontario M1P 2E7

Van Nostrand Reinhold Australia Pty. Ltd.
17 Queen Street, Mitcham, Victoria 3132

Van Nostrand Reinhold Company Ltd.
Molly Millars Lane, Wokingham, Berkshire, England RG11 2PY

Cloth edition published 1975 by Van Nostrand Reinhold Company

16 15 14 13 12 11 10 9 8 7 6 5 4 3 2 1

Contents

Foreword

In the beginning was the sign.

All peoples in all times and in all places have applied these signs in thousands of variations and combinations.

The sign became a symbol. "A symbol is a word or sign whenever it 'means' more than one sees at first glance" (C.G. Jung). The sign acquires a deeper meaning and takes the place of an abstract idea.

becomes a symbol for the sun.

becomes a symbol for water.

The vertical line symbolizes man walking erect, the manly; the tree growing tall; the bond between heaven and earth, the spiritual and the material.

The horizontal line symbolizes resting, sleeping, dead man; the felled tree; the earth, the material, the passive.

The two great contrasts united in one sign had been adapted everywhere before the Crucifixion of Christ; after that time it became the holy symbol of Christ, the sign of love and goodness.

The swastika was an ornamental sign known to the old Chinese, the Babylonians, and the Mayas in America.

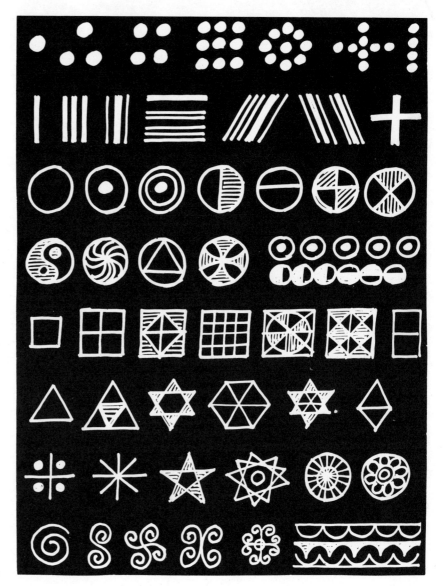

Fig. I-1.

Playing with the signs rhythmically led to ornament. Fig. I-1 shows basic forms of elementary ornamentation, on which endless variations have been made in the course of the centuries.

The ornament could again become a symbol (see the illustrations in Chapter 2).

Sign, symbol, ornament—three connected elements and a closely knit trilogy.

Ornament is "in" again in our time. In spite of ostracization in the past, ornament is blooming as never before. Young people today have used ornament and color to make a happier, more pleasurable world.

Man is a "seeing animal": the most plentiful and the most direct information comes via our eyes and our brains to our consciousness. Our world is becoming more and more a visual world: letters and signs, emblems, trademarks, signals, pictures, news, and other means of communication in all forms and colors threaten to overwhelm us.

The modern world is becoming small. On our television screens we see pictures and news reports from all over the world, "live" and in color; jet airplanes bring us in a few hours to any part of the world. A large part of the population uses the same letter signs. The only handicap to world communication is the thousands of different languages. A world language is still far away, but a general international sign language is closer to realization. The increasing world traffic needs it badly. International traffic signs for automobiles and similar indications for trains, airports, harbors, stations, etc., are urgently needed. The sign rules the world.

Sign, symbol, and ornament: the meaningful triad, the closely knit triptych to which this book will bear witness in words and pictures. The theme is wide-spreading and all-embracing.

The emphasis is on the subject of ornamentation, the art of decorating which flows deep in man's blood and is a part of his being. Clear and precise definitions will be attempted by means of words and pictures, to give the buyer a basis for better judgment of the many "decorated" products available and to provide guidelines for the many people who like to make and decorate things in their free time.

Introduction

In early civilizations ornament arose from peaceful occupation without any thought of monetary gain; it was a meaningful symbolic language laden with magic powers. Above and beyond the symbolic content there was undoubtedly the joy of rhythmic decoration itself. Whether it be a pitcher from the Stone Ages or a dish from the ancient Asiatic or Greek cultures, symbol and decoration have quite clearly been the driving forces behind ornament. Over thousands of years, particularly in the development of European styles since the beginning of recorded history, the original, simple, elementary forms have broadened into a rich stream of ornamental tradition. Generally speaking, they have lost not only their simplicity but also their expressive power and symbolic meaning in modern times.

According to the concepts of each particular period, artists and artisans have constantly discovered new possibilities in ornamental expression. In trying to review its development (there is as yet, unfortunately, no complete history of form and style in ornament), we discover a rich and blossoming world, a source of inexhaustible beauty, which is an integral part of the history of the fine arts: the strong, massive forms of the Carolingian and Romanesque periods; the significant, straight lines of Gothic art, the decorative forms of the Renaissance; the rich fullness and dynamic extravagance of the Baroque period; the luxuriant, florid splendor of the Rococo age, which introduced asymmetric lines into ornamentation for the first time; and the exhilarating field of folk art.

In our own time only the Jugendstil was able to create its own ornamental form, in which the undulating line played an important role. It was all a little feeble, however, and it petered out in decadent flourishes that lacked real meaning or impact.

Our generation, in fact, has only just discovered the magnificence of the so-called primitive cultures. In the Paris of the young Picasso and Braque, African masks and sculpture had the impact of thunder. The way to the ornamental wonders of Oceania, Melanesia, Africa, and the old Indian cultures of America was opened. And what have we learned from them? Do we find an echo in the work of today? Perhaps our modern curtain materials are the only field in which the suggestive, primitive power of the Asmatic art of New Guinea, for example, finds an echo. Certainly, present-day architecture and industrial design have no idea about how to cope with the problems of color and decoration on buildings.

Whenever I see the work of Buckminister Fuller or Nervi, who have been able in certain buildings to achieve the clean nobility found in a ship's propeller or a modern jet fighter, I have the feeling that these artists, together with nature, which builds crystals, seashells, and structures, can show us a way to a new world where form, ornament, and color combine into one indivisible organic whole, a condition which used to be present in things made by human hands. The problem of ornamentation and decoration preoccupies not only everyone engaged in the field of design but also everyone who takes a critical look at the world around him.

It is a good idea to study ornament in its original context in order to understand the relationship between man and ornament and to delve into the subconscious and the primeval.

In ornamentation it is possible to trace the history of mankind from the very beginning. Man is as clearly evident in tools and artifacts as in the great paintings in Lascaux or the ancient writings we are endeavoring to decipher.

Ornamentation is at the same time the imprint of man. Early history does not reveal its secrets easily. We shall never know why one man came to paint a bison on a cave wall while another formed a voluptuous female statue of clay and another made markings on gravel stones from the river. Was it a woman who made the first symbol for waves in the form of a serpentine line; was it a snake or the curving lines of her own body that inspired her to do so; who was the "discoverer" of the zigzag line that has been endlessly repeated and modified? We shall never know!

Man's need for ornamentation, which has been amply evidenced through the centuries by all peoples everywhere, can be traced back to his fundamental bond with the world that surrounds him. Seen in this light, ornamentation is the natural handwriting of mankind: it comes from his life rhythms. As soon as he makes his experiences visible, ornament is created. No other pattern can be created, because man experiences life and his ties with nature as a movement, a rhythm. The changes of day into night, the seasons, the throb of his heatbeat, his breathing, the sequence of movements that follow one another, the harmonious movement of wind and water, of sun and moon and stars in their celestial courses—they are all evidence of nature, of which man himself is a part. And it is against this objective order of things that we should measure our judgments about ornamentation.

12

To deny man's deep and eternal desire to use ornament is to deny an anthropological phenomenon. To isolate this need from the context of objective norms is to reduce ornament to a superficial decoration, which can no longer be experienced as a living and organic force.

True ornament is as old as man himself: it springs from man's need for play and rhythmic repetition. It is evident in all peoples, independently of one another, and it has been present since prehistoric times.

Even more remarkable is the fact that the basic forms of elementary ornamentation are the same the world over and in all ages: the same simple symbolism and principles recur. The word "ornament" comes from the Latin *ornare,* to decorate something, and *ordinare,* to order. Le Corbusier says: "Decoration is a questionable matter, but pure, simple ornamentation is like a sign: it is a synthesis, an experience of an order! 'Ornament' making is a categorical discipline."

I have already said that ornamentation also developed from man's joy in his work—his pleasure in adding luster, value, or a more opulent appearance. Because of his need to crown an object and to decorate it in a festive manner, man has been using ornamentation ever since he began to make things. He decorates them in order to value them more highly. A good ornament was always the result of intensive work and at the same time a proof of caring and of his artistic ability.

Joy in ornamentation cannot be separated from the thought of skillful human hands. And a part of the living power that emanates from true ornamentation stems from what was put into it during its execution.

Ornament finds its roots in magic and symbolism—its origin is the two-in-oneness of man and the cosmos, of which he himself is the mirror.

Ornamentation, myth and symbol in the beginning, has been gradually secularized: the finial on the Gothic spire and the rose windows in the cathedrals of Chartres, Amiens, and Strasbourg were symbols and myths. But the misuse and abuse of true ornamentation in the industrial age is no reason to discard it completely.

PART I. SIGNS

Fig. 1-1. Runic signs. The origin and development of runic signs is not certain: until about 500 A.D. certain signs were used in the Germanic countries, first as cult signs and as letters.

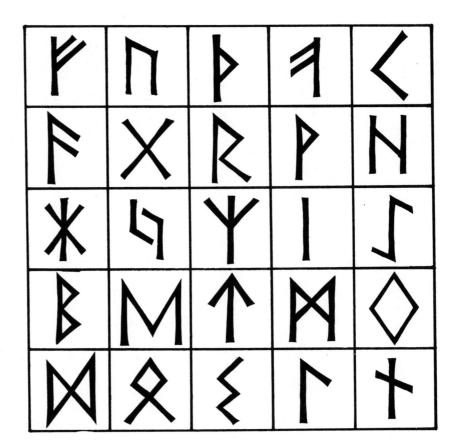

1. Old Signs

In their origins signs are suggestive of the mystic, the mysterious, the secret and private. They have existed from prehistoric times, as we know from evidence on the cave walls where the first human beings lived and from the first objects that they made.

Signs are still used today in their original forms by groups of people who live outside the mainstream of ordered, established society—thieves, beggars, gypsies—who put secret signs on walls, doors, fences, and trees. There are, moreover, living secret languages that fit into this category. Secret, religious, and mysterious elements have largely disappeared in the present-day world, but the number of signs has increased enormously.

The meaning of the old signs has more or less disappeared. Reason and intellect predominate: dreams, imagination, mystery—things that dwell in the deeper regions of the human spirit—have lost their value for most people. The *sign* as a world-wide means of communication, however, is increasing in importance, and man is developing all kinds of graphic images that can be understood by large groups of people. Modern man treks all over the world on business—to festivals, congresses, Olympic games, and many other pursuits. We have to learn a language of signs that can take us anywhere. For this reason careful attention has been paid to modern signs in this book.

Here is a list of various applications of letters, signs, and signals: information boards, knot writing, runic signs, cave signs, pictographs (picture signs), tally-stick signs, cuneiform writing, hieroglyphics; signs for the hand, for the fingers (for the deaf), footprint writing for the blind (Braille); house signs, monograms, tokens, ownership signs, numbers; letters, ciphers, musical notation, Morse code, boundary stones, place-name boards; guild signs, handwork signs, trademarks; communication signs for journeys, in hotels, on airfields, at stations, in harbors, on highways, in cities, etc; signs for international congresses, Olympic games, festivals; traffic signs, identification plates for automobiles, airfields, ships, etc.; signs on equipment, switchboards and keyboards in industry, churches, offices; playing cards, constellations, cartographic signs, zodiac signs, flags, standards, banners, factory, firm, and industry signs; stamps of all kinds (postal, customs, traffic, etc.); membership signs, emblems; military-rank signs; signals for shipping traffic; light signals, illuminated advertisements, poster and cinema advertisements, highway advertisements, advertising, and other visual means of communication.

Terms and Concepts

Sign: visual gesture or picture (figure) that indicates a certain content, thought, or thing.

Symbol: sign, token, or emblem that expresses a meaning not directly deducible from the sign but recognizable only to those who have learned it.

Emblem: sign or token that expresses a concrete form of an abstract content: particularly a sign for a union, club, foundation, group, community, etc.

Signal: conveyor of information or of a sign (color, light, movement, gesture, etc.).

Mark: sign (factory trademark, product trademark, quality trademark) that signifies a particular business, company, firm, or product and is placed on the product or the packaging as well as on all means of communication (letterheads, notes, advertisements, stamps, etc.).

Insignia (or *colophon*): originally a sign of a printer or publisher, later a wider meaning; a mark with a simple composition (a single letter or other figure), as a trademark, image, or display sign for an industry, business, shop, etc.

Pictograph: depiction in a sign of articles or things (Egyptian hieroglyphics)—a kind of writing developed from a simplification of the real picture.

Information: not a sign but an indication of an abstract idea (e.g., flashing light at a railway crossing).

From the development of cybernetics (the science of communications control) and the enormous need for efficient world communication and information, specializations have been developed in the field of sign knowledge that have given rise to a great deal of discussion and publicity.

Semiotics: the science and theory of signs in general: a general and linguistic theory of signs.

Semantics: that part of semiotics that concerns itself with the definition and explanation of the content and meaning of abstract signs and sign systems.

Pragmatics: that part of semiotics that concerns itself with the origin, application, and effect of signs.

Syntactics: that part of semiotics that concerns itself with a particular sign as a means or intermediary of the sign as such (not its actual meaning).

Informatics: the theory and science of modern information and documentation, which make use of the preceding sciences. Together, these disciplines open the way to a world language of signs, for which there is an international need. The enormous growth of world communication and the expanding use of computers make this an urgent necessity.

Fig. 1-2. Monograms. A monogram is a sign composed of letter forms derived from the name (first and/or last name) of the person concerned. Monograms have always played an important role in the world of signs, and man seems to derive pleasure from playing with the letters of his name and combining them into an attractive design, sometimes with a hidden meaning. Among the most beautiful are the Byzantine monograms, which combine power and monumentality with dignity and seriousness. These famous examples are from the *Book of Signs* by Rudolf Koch. The following monograms are illustrated, starting on the top row from left to right: Charlemagne; Paleologus; Emperor Justinian; unknown, with Christ symbol; unknown; Aerobindus; Emperor Otto the Great; the name "Johannes"; Bishop Arethras of Caesarea.

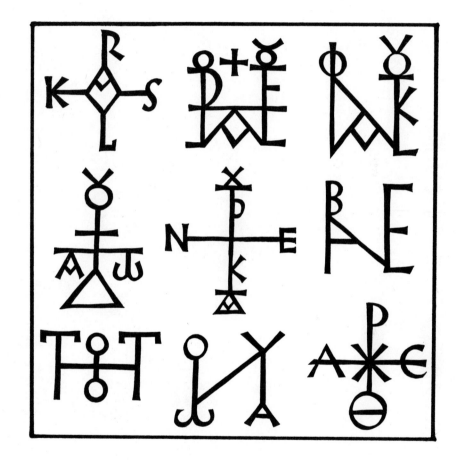

Figs. 1-3 and 1-4. Rock engravings from Val Camonica (northern Italy) from different eras of the Neolithic Age—before 2200 B.C.—to the Ice Age (roughly the time of Christ's birth). These drawings were made from photographs and rubbings made by students of the Kunstgewerbeschule in Zurich. They are geometric pictographs illustrating how early man, who had made the transition from wandering hunter and forager to established farmer, set down his thoughts and his concept of the world in expressive symbols and signs. These particular examples can be augmented by thousands more from all over the world.

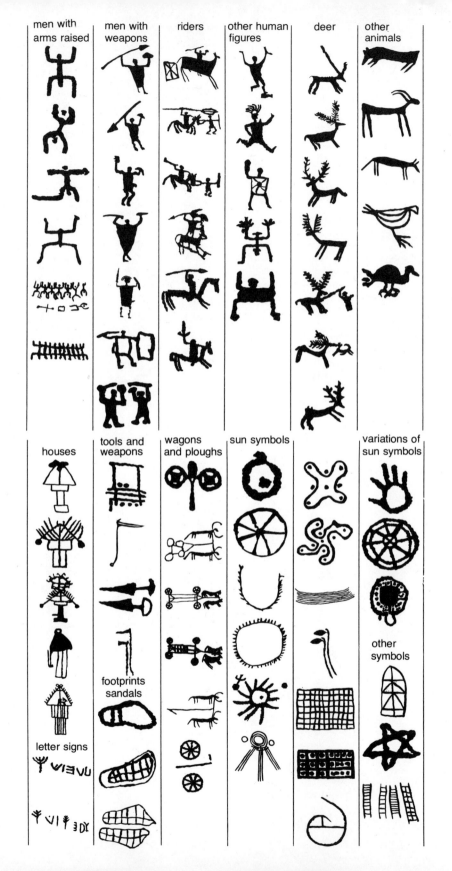

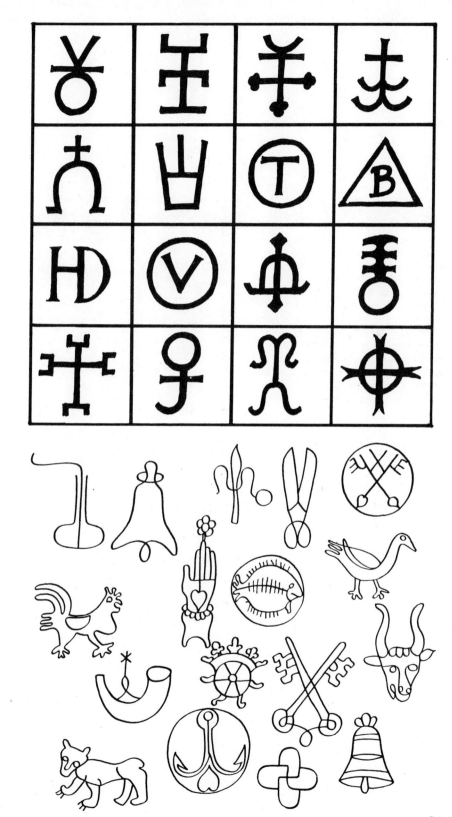

Fig. 1-5. Old branding signs for cattle. The history of branding signs goes back to the culture of the nomadic cattle farmers; pedigree and herd signs are still used even today. These old signs were often family or tribal signs as well; they are very beautiful and mysterious, somewhat reminiscent of old runic letters.

Fig. 1-6. Watermarks on handmade paper. A watermark is a kind of mark (letter, cypher, symbol, figure, etc.) that is put onto the paper during its manufacture in order to indicate its origin (factory mark) or to prevent its imitation (on money or valuable documents). Genuine watermarks are fabricated at the same time as the paper by imposing the outline of the mark on the paper sieve. The mark becomes visible on the thinner parts of the paper where there is less pulp.

Fig. 1-7. Man has always taken the course of the sun as a standard for the periodic division of time, and for this reason the fixed constellations of the zodiac are important. The first system of division dates from the Sumerians, 23 centuries B.C. The circular shape of the zodiac dates from the 14th century. Since then the circle—in which the movement of the moon and planets also took place—has been divided into twelve parts with twelve constellations. Thus each sign occupies 30 degrees. This drawing illustrates the signs of the zodiac with their correct dates.

2. Letter Signs

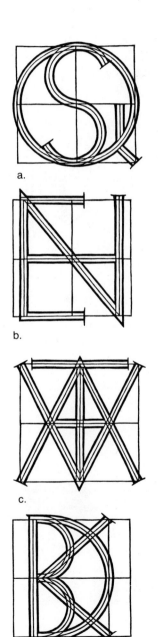

a.

b.

c.

d.

Alphabet letters must be classified in the category of signs and symbols and also, surely, in the category of ornament. Among the most classical and beautiful alphabets are the Roman capitals, shown in fig. 2-1 in their relationship to each other and to the square.

Letters are not only an indispensable collection of signs for visual communication but also a collection of stimulating forms that present a challenge to be manipulated and played with.

Nowadays, there are many different sorts of letters in use. All of them have one or more standard forms and many variations on them—the simple, common types and the more ornamental versions for festive occasions. There are both handwritten letters and machine letters, while the computer letter is in the process of development. The assortment of different typefaces and sizes of machine letters at our disposal is almost limitless.

The typical ornamental letters of past centuries are back in style and are being readapted by graphic designers; hand lettering no longer exists, and we no longer have a writing culture like the Japanese and Chinese. Fig. 2-2 illustrates on the left a number of more or less decorative letters from our normal alphabet; above right, an example of folk letter art, which the ornamentation makes practically illegible; below right, an example of an ornamental page from the Koran, with an invocation to the patron of the Dervishes. Many magnificently executed and often very large letter proverbs can be found in the mosques of the East.

The Jugendstil, or "Youth Style," named after the Munich newspaper "Youth," has also left its mark on letters and book design. Typical of this style, which was strongly based on art needlework (influenced by the Arts and Crafts movement led by Ruskin and Morris in England), was a linear, ornamental treatment of planes and a particular preference for flowing plant-and-flower motifs.

The letter types of Morris are the first examples of this new form and spirit. Otto Eckmann was the most outspoken German calligrapher. The Eckmann alphabet still bears traces of the Youth Style.

Fig. 2-1. (a.) Letters O, C, G, Q, and S. (b.) Letters E, L, F, H, and N. (c.) Letters I, T, A, and V. (d.) Letters P, B, R, K, and D.

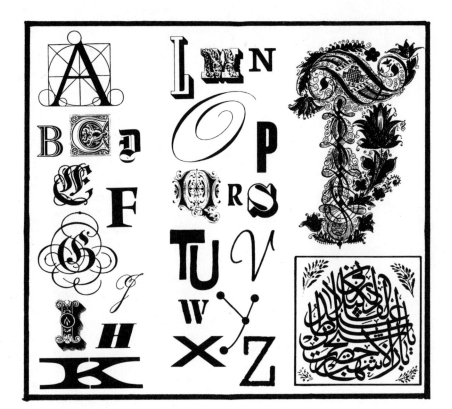

Fig. 2-2.

Fig. 2-3. Magnificent examples of Islamic calligraphy hang on the interior walls of mosques, often spelling out in large, ornamental forms the word "Allah" or excerpts from the Koran. These examples show straight, stylized letter forms rather than decorative writing. They are read beginning at bottom right.

Fig. 2-4. The imagination of the Irish monks is best exemplified in the ornamental pages of the *Book of Kells and the Evangelical Book of Lindisfarne*. Unique transformations of the letters combine with Irish band ornament and beautiful colors to create a work of magical splendor.

a.

rex iudeorum. Hunc ergo titulum multi legerunt
iudeorum quia prope ciuitatem erat locus ubi cruci-
fixus est iesus: et erat scriptum hebraice grece et la-
tine. Dicebant ergo pilato pontifices iudeorum.
Noli scribere rex iudeorum sed quia ipse dixit. Rex
sum iudeorum. Respondit pilatus. Quod scripsi
scripsi. Milites ergo cum crucifixissent eum acceper-
unt uestimenta eius et fecerunt quatuor partes uni-
cuique militi partem et tunicam. Erat autem tunica inco-
sutilis desuper contexta per totum. Dixerunt ergo
ad inuicem. Non scindamus eam sed sortiamur
de illa cuius sit: ut scriptura impleretur dicens.
Partiti sunt uestimenta mea sibi et in ueste mea
miserunt sortem. Et milites quidem hec fecerunt.
Stabat autem iuxta crucem iesu mater eius et so-
ror matris eius maria cleophe et maria mag-
dalene. Cum uidisset ergo iesus matrem et dis-
cipulum stantem quem diligebat: dixit matri
sue. Mulier ecce filius tuus. Deinde dixit dis-
cipulo. Ecce mater tua. Et ex illa hora accepit
eam discipulus in sua. Postea sciens iesus
quia omnia consumata sunt: ut consumaretur
scriptura dixit. Sitio. Vas autem positum erat
aceto plenum. Illi autem spongiam plenam aceto

b.

Liber generationis iesu christi
filii dauid: filii abraham.
Abraham genuit ysaac:
ysaac autem genuit iacob.
Jacob autem genuit iudam et fratres eius:
iudas autem genuit phares et zaram de
thamar. Phares autem genuit esrom:
esrom autem genuit aram. Aram autem
genuit aminadab: aminadab autem genuit naason. Naason autem genuit salomon: salomon autem genuit booz de raab.
Booz autem genuit obeth ex ruth: obeth
autem genuit iesse. Jesse autem genuit dauid regem: dauid autem rex genuit salo-
monem ex ea que fuit urie. Salomon autem
genuit roboam: roboam autem genuit
abyam. Abyas autem genuit asa: asa
autem genuit iosaphat. Josaphat autem
genuit ioram: ioram autem genuit oziam. Ozias autem genuit ioatham: ioatham autem genuit achat. Achar autem
genuit ezechiam: ezechias autem genuit
manassen: manasses autem genuit ammon. Ammon autem genuit iosiam:

Fig. 2-5. (a.) Handwriting from a 15th-century missal. (b.) Reprint of the missal handwriting by Gutenberg.

Fig. 2-6. (a.) Ornamental letter drawn by Paul Franck in 1601. (b.) Ornamental-letter labyrinth, woodcut by I. C. Hiltensperger at the beginning of the 18th century.

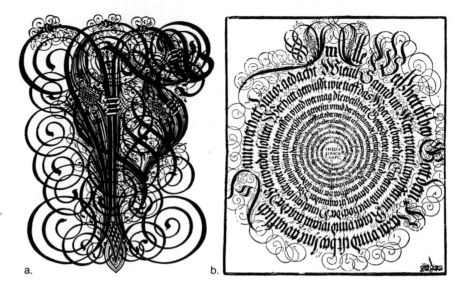

a.

b.

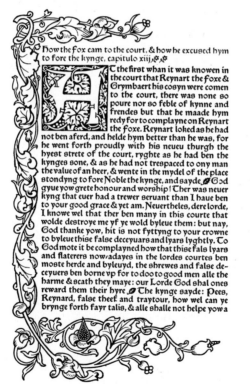

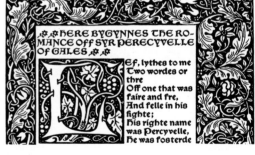

Fig. 2-7. In the 1890s William Morris consciously rejected the neohistorical forms then dominating composition and returned to the original writing forms and techniques of incunabula, thereby introducing a new style of book printing.

Fig. 2-8. In the 17th century copperplate engraving began to be used in calligraphy. The aim was to make the writing appear "cut." This type of letter was used to decorate crystal goblets. The attractive lines were achieved by increased or decreased pressure on the pen.

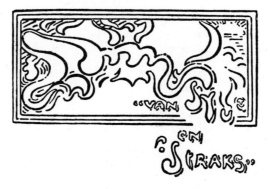

Fig. 2-9. Title page from the Flemish newspaper *Van Nu en Straks*, designed by Henry van de Velde in 1893.

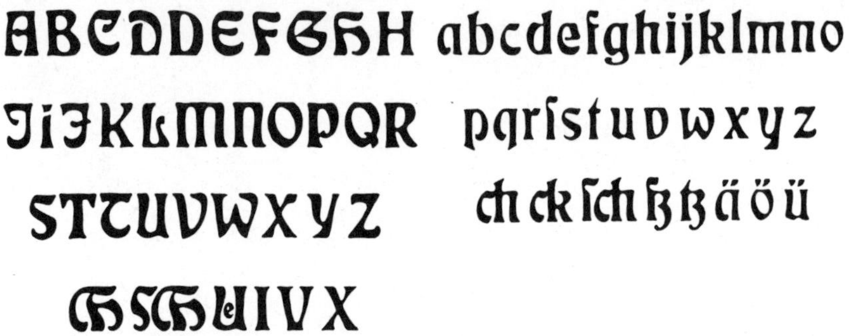

ABCDDEFGHH abcdefghijklmno
JiFKLMNOPQR pqrstuvwxyz
STTUVWXYZ ch ck sch ß ß ä ö ü
CH SCH UIVX

Fig. 2-10. Otto Eckmann's alphabet, developed circa 1900.

Fig. 2-11. Three examples of the German Jugendstil by Bernhard Pankok, Otto Eckmann, and Peter Behrens.

Fig. 2-12. Initial drawn by Otto Eckmann for Rudhard, a type foundry, circa 1900.

Fig. 2-13. The Dutch Youth Style at its best: some beautiful vignettes cut in wood by G. W. Dijsselhof.

Fig. 2-14. Lithographed prospectus cover by Johan Thorn Prikker, 1897. (Collection of the Municipal Archives, The Hague.)

Fig. 2-15. A Russian poem by El Lissitski (one of the best-known constructivists, who introduced new ideas and techniques in architecture, painting, and graphics), graphically and ornamentally composed in 1923.

Fig. 2-16. A typographical composition (1924) by the Groningen artist-printer Hendrik N. Werkman. His work consisted mostly of prints with graphic material in primary colors.

een waarborg voor betrouwbaarheid wenscht ge?

de **n.k.f** maakte in de

18

jaar van haar bestaan

millioenen meters kabel die absoluut voldeden

n.v. nederlandsche kabelfabriek **n.k.f delft**

Figs. 2-17 and 2-18. Piet Zwart is noted for his early experiments with ornamental typography for business purposes. These two pieces are advertisements.

LAGA=
COMPAGNIE
HAAG
ANNA PAULOWNASTRAAT 47
TELEFOON Nos HAAG 916
MARNIX 916

=IOCO=
RUBBER=
VLOEREN

Fig. 2-19. The sign "dead," executed by the great Zen master Hakuin (1768–1865) from Kyoto. He added a note to the sign, which said, "Whenever anyone understands this, then he is out of danger." The connection between letter and image is at its strongest in Zen calligraphy.

Fig. 2-20. A page from the catalog of the UNESCO Exhibition "Die Kunst der Schrift," held in 1964. The a was cut by the French printer Garamond (1480–1561). The other sign represents "hero" and was cut by the Japanese calligrapher Inone Yuichi in 1961.

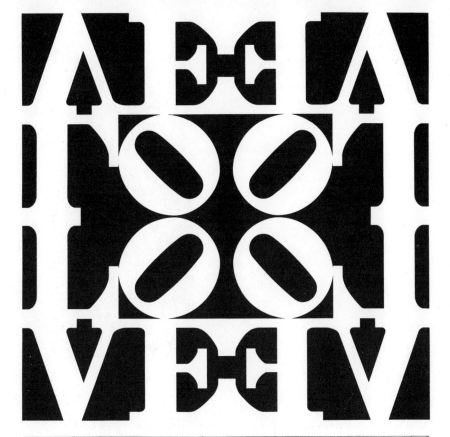

Fig. 2-21. A letter composition by Robert Indiana entitled *Black and White Love* (1971). It has strongly ornamental overtones—especially the many-sided symmetry and the extreme contrast of black and white. Indiana's work consists largely of compositions with letters and figures.

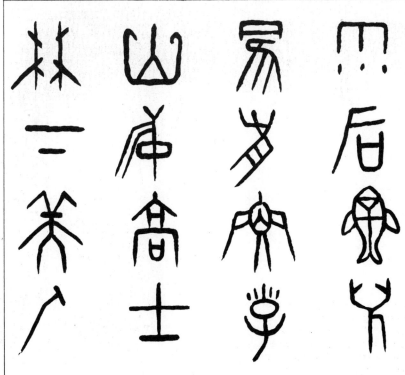

Fig. 2-22. Picture writing by Wu Cheng-Yan, a painter and calligrapher from Taipei (Formosa). It is a series of picture signs and cryptographs, which clearly predict the future.

Fig. 2-23. A sign designed by Dick Eiffers for the Bijenkorf Company, 1971. Bert Schierbeek has written a poem to accompany it: "A script full of streets of kings, with the guitar of the night in our heart."

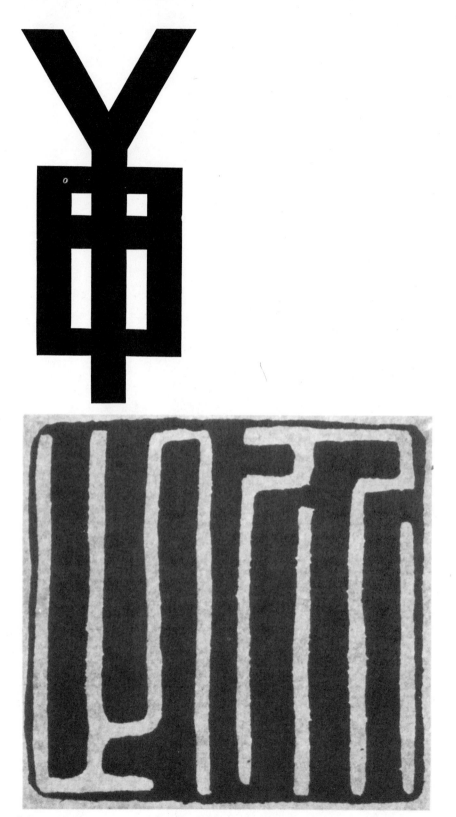

Figs. 2-24 and 2-25. Two signs from the house publication of Merchanische Web-erei Pausa. The first has a letterlike character; the second is specifically a letter sign, composed of "fashionable" elements.

Fig. 2-26. In 1928 Chinese archae-
ologists discovered the graves of the
Shang dynasty (1450–1000 B.C.). They
found 300 graves, 1,100 skeletons,
weapons, tools, jewels, ceramics and the
famous bronzes. Many of these articles
were decorated with written signs like
these, the oldest evidence of writing in
East Asia. The script and the writing were
later elevated to a high art: according to a
Japanese proverb, "To be a master of
writing is to be a real man."

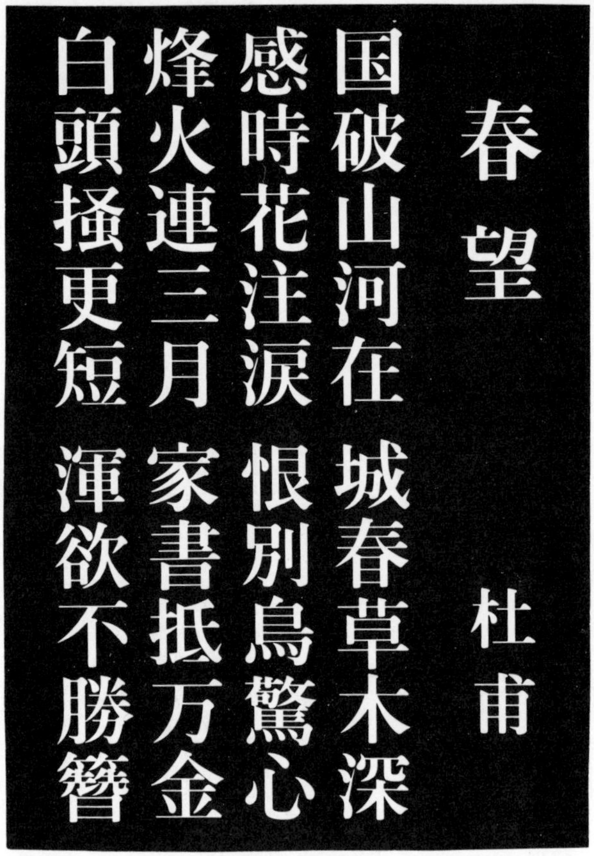

春望

杜甫

国破山河在 城春草木深
感時花濺淚 恨別鳥驚心
烽火連三月 家書抵万金
白頭掻更短 渾欲不勝簪

Fig. 2-27. Different types of Chinese writing.

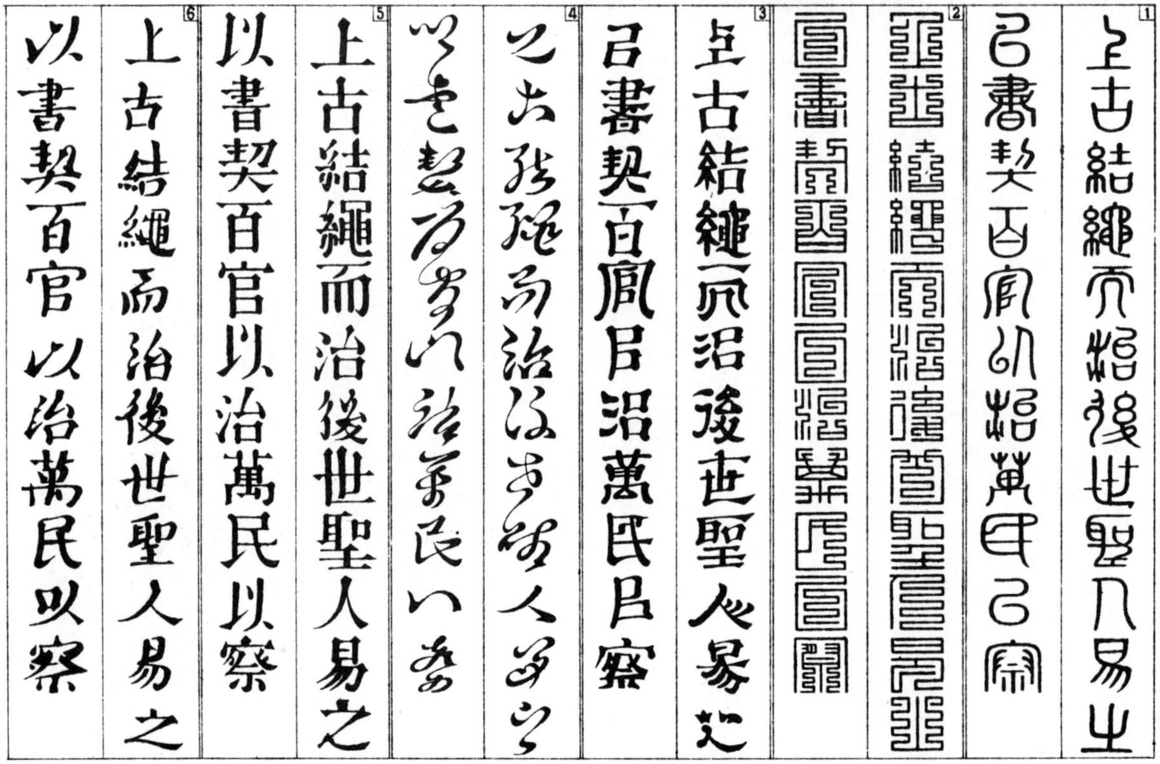

36

Fig. 2-28. Collection of stars designed by the employees of Grafistas Agripacion, a Spanish graphics firm. The designs show how a strictly geometric form can be transformed into freely geometric ornaments.

3. Coats of Arms, Trademarks, & Traffic Signs

Fig. 3-1. Composite of a number of different signs from the *Symbol Source Book*, edited by Henry Dreyfuss.

Figs. 3-2 and 3-3. The human figure as sign, symbol, and ornament in Olympic signs and Egyptian hieroglyphics. One of the slogans of our time is "visual communications," hence the concepts of semiotics (general theory of signs) and semantics (the relationship between an object and its sign—the meaning of the sign). As a result of intensified international traffic, it is imperative to have an international sign language. These picture signs are also called "pictographs." Fig. 3-2 shows symbols and signs for the different sports at the Munich Olympic Games, 1972. Fig. 3-3a shows the basic figure and the blueprint. Fig. 3-3b is a sample of comparable signs for the Tokyo Olympic Games, 1964. Fig. 3-3c indicates the Egyptian hieroglyphs for speaking, woman, carrying, drinking, and rowing, respectively. They date from circa 3000 B.C.

a.

b.

c.

39

Fig. 3-4. International travel signs as interpreted in the "house style" of the Dutch Railways (designed by Tel-design).

 entrance

 exit

 information

 coffee shop

 taxi

 restaurant

 automat

 toilet

 ladies' room

 parking

 mens' room

 baggage depot

 baggage dispatch

 lockers

 flowers

 waiting room

 lost and found

 hairdresser

 bicycle dispatch

 general baggage

Fig. 3-5. Traffic and information signs designed by students.

 entrance

 exit

 no smoking

 do not touch

 danger

 ladies' room

 mens' room

 fire alarm

 telephone

 mailbox

 police

 doctor

 hospital

 drugstore

 information

 exchange office

 gas station

 station

airport

harbor

hotel

museum

monument

direction sign

Fig. 3-6. Pictographic traffic signs along a bicycle path. Traffic signs are instantly recognizable to all travelers without further explanation. Sign/symbol language has been most regulated in this particular field, both in form and in color. Geometric forms (circles, triangles, squares) and basic colors (red, blue, yellow) plus black and white are primarily used. In this way these signs acquire an ornamental character.

Fig. 3-7. These simple, expressive, graphic signs, marking divisions of a plane, were designed to be seen quickly and at a great distance in order to identify a Japanese ship and its company. This example of an ornamental, geometric sign language is comparable to traffic signs.

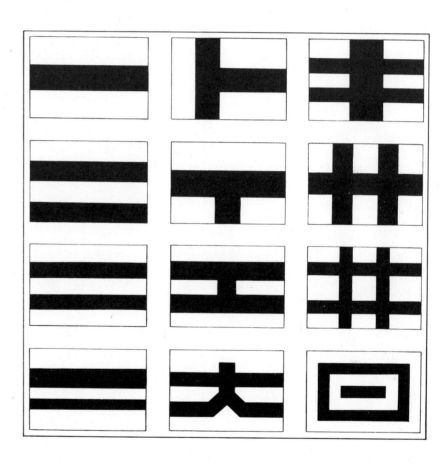

Fig. 3-8. Municipal coats of arms, all featuring the eagle. Coats of arms, colors, and standards were first used in China and Japan and were adopted in Europe in the Middle Ages. Originally the emblems for families and public bodies, their use has been extended to include supranational organizations.

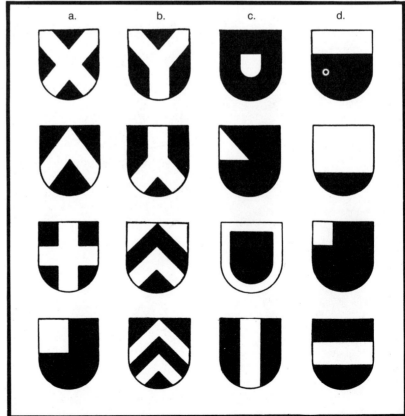

Fig. 3-9. When emblems began to be depicted on shields, heraldry came into being. Precise rules were established regulating forms, divisions, and colors, each with their own names and meanings. Principal heraldic emblems are shown here: (a.) St. Andrews' cross, chevron, cross, free quarter; (b.) pall, inverted pall, couple-close, chevronel; (c.) heart shield, gusset, bordure, pale; (d.) chief, foot, canton, fess.

Fig. 3-10. Japanese family coats of arms.

There are certain words in the Japanese language that cannot be directly translated into English, one of which is *katachi*. It is usually translated as "form," but in fact it has a wider meaning. It expresses the art of giving form to one's total surroundings—to bring about functional and even spiritual happiness.

The origin of this concept lies in Japanese religion, and the spirit of Buddhism still leaves its mark on daily life—household, utensils, and the Zen etiquette of the tea ceremony.

All the forms must be simple but of the highest perfection. The refined movements reveal the chastity and purity of all things. Forms and traditional patterns rule the life of the Japanese. From the 6th to the 19th century there were three groups in Japanese society: the nobility and the samurai (warriors), the merchants in the cities, and the farmers on the land. Each of these groups developed its own forms and traditions. The family coat of arms—the *moncho*—first developed among the samurai class. Later it appeared on the houses of the merchants and then on the sides of the farmers' barns, on their clothing, and on their tools. These coats of arms, or signs, designed with the greatest care and taste, were to play a great role in the life of the Japanese, and they are part of the concept *katachi*.

The peak of this refined language of form was reached in the middle of the Edo period (second half of the 17th century to the end of the 18th century). The refinement and cultivation of family signs find parallels in the high cultures of sword guards *(tsubas)* and girdle knots *(netsukes)* and in the forging of the sword itself.

The ornamentation of the *tsubas,* which later became collectors' items both in Japan and abroad, is an art of the highest order, from which Japanese ornamentation has descended through the centuries (see fig. 12-5).

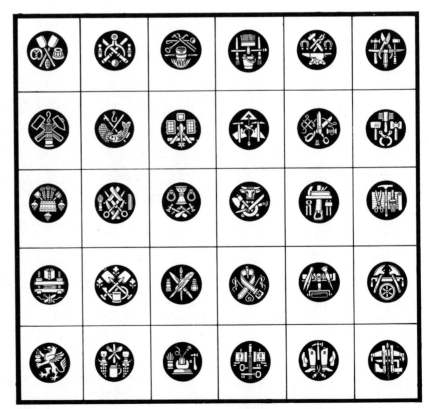

Fig. 3-11. Signs for handwork, trades, and professions designed by graphic artists Kredel, Hampe, and Wolpe for the Bauersche Giesserei Company.

44

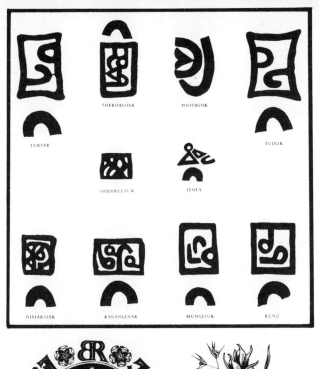

Fig. 3-12. Eskimo name signs, made by cutting small plastics from soapstone. Eskimos also made stone engravings (see figs. 10-16 and 10-17). The semi-circles under the signs indicate that they were made in the artist's igloo.

Fig. 3-13. Bookmarks also belong to the category of signs. They are usually wood engravings, miniature masterpieces of graphic workmanship in which the name is ornamentally intertwined with reference to profession or field of importance. These examples were designed by Dirk van Gelder (b., c., d., g., h., i.) and Pam Rueter (a., e., f.).

Fig. 3-14. Trademarks based on motifs from nature. Designed by: (a) Ward and Saks, Inc. for Jack Lenor Larsen; (b.) Vogtel, book printers; (c.) Bror Zetterberg for Turun Kala Oy, fish canners; (d.) Stefan Kantscheff for Centrum van Industriele Vormgeving; (e.) Stefan Kantscheff for a meat-importing-and-exporting company; (f.) Chris Yaneff for an artificial-manure firm; (g.) Eiko Pech for Rheumatic Center; (h.) Klaus Grözinger and Klaus Nothdruft for a wine-importing firm; (i.) Louis le Brouguy for a silk-spinning firm; (j.) Hans Schleger for Mac Fisheries; (k.) Hansman and Langford for British Eagle International Airways; (l.) Klaus Grözinger for the School of Youth Group Leaders; (m.) David Stanfield for Sparta; (n.) Milton Glazer for the Golden Snail restaurant; (o.) Michael Russell for Lyons Bakery; (p.) F.H.K. Henrion for the Square Grip steel and concrete company.

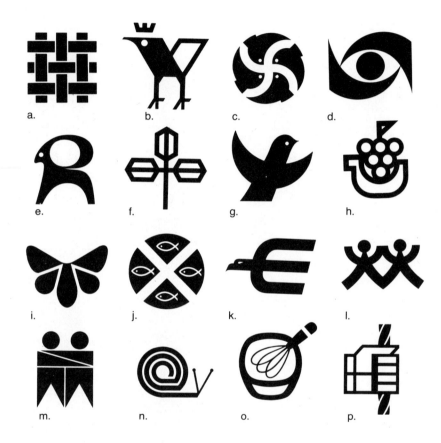

Fig. 3-15. Cover of the annual report of the Irish design center Kilkenny Workshops. The designer has composed this ornamental page from signs and symbols that indicate the insignias of the Kilkenny Workshops and the product groups they manufacture: textiles, wood turning, ceramics, and metal castings. By outlining all the motifs with a thick circle and arranging them in a square, he has created a good ornamental page.

Figs. 3-16 and 3-17. The larger European farmers used to have signs, marks, or coats of arms printed, often in color, on the sacks in which their grain was brought to the mills. The printing blocks were cut by the printers themselves from pearwood, using their imagination whenever the name of the farmer or his region did not directly suggest a motif. The stamp in fig. 3-16 is shown full-scale; fig. 3-17 shows a number of sack stamps reduced in size.

PART II. SYMBOLS

4. Old & New Meanings

The modern realistic school of thought has turned away from things that used to have a great significance in the life of mankind: dreams, imagination, fantasy. Sober understanding, doubt, the machine, the computer, and the intellect have taken their place.

The symbol as a poetic game is a thing of the past. Even the Christian symbols, which sustained and inspired mankind for so many centuries, have lost their meaning. Other signs have been made into symbols. Modern thinking has deviated more and more from ancient thought since the Renaissance.

Ancient and medieval thinking perceived external manifestations of the world as real only insofar as a higher, godlike truth was expressed in them: the things of the world were merely reflections of higher, more complete forms of existence. These higher forms are true reality, primeval pictures, eternal thoughts. Only together—worldly things and eternal truth—was the whole reality of heaven and earth manifested.

The primeval meaning of a symbol is thus a *recognition sign,* or other half. An example is the half of a ring given by a host to his guest in order that they might recognize each other, even after many years. A symbol, therefore, is a thing of this world, which in itself is nothing, just as the half of the ring is nothing: it fits the other half, the divine idea, which alone can give it full reality. It is necessary to recognize the idea behind every thing: the symbol is only half of the truth.

Christianity, heir to this ancient attitude, has bequeathed to us in its artistic and liturgical language a large number of meaningful symbols, which show us how surely and lovingly the spirit of man penetrated into the being and the mystery of things.

In the late Middle Ages and the Renaissance these symbols—once full of life and deep meaning—stultified and shriveled up into allegories. An allegory comes into being whenever a concrete image takes the place of an abstract thought, e.g., a child stands for youth; a white-bearded old man, for old age; an owl on a book, for wisdom; a skeleton, for the dead; or an hourglass, for the passage of time.

A symbol, on the other hand, moves the deep, secret recesses of the human soul. A symbol is directed inwards; an allegory, outwards. Symbols carry the mind over the borders of the finite into the realm of the infinite. They give rise to conjecture, speculation—they are the signs of the unspeakable. A symbol does not always have to be a sign: it can be a color or a sound or a word. I have tried in this short chapter to shed some light on the subject of old (yet always new) signs, which are still relevant to our times. Without a deeper understanding of the old signs and symbols, it is not possible to penetrate into the soul of works of art, much less share in the creative process itself.

5. General Symbols: Meaning & Significance

Following are descriptions of some common symbols. All of them are shown consecutively in figs. 5-1 and 5-2.

Point: the primeval element, beginning, and kernel; symbol of the number. It is the symbol of the beginning (grain of seed) and of the end (grain of dust); it represents the smallest substance (atom, nucleus). The point is in fact imaginary: it occupies no space. In ornamentation and sign art the point or dot sometimes becomes a small, filled-in circle. In writing and typography the point has the meaning of "stop, new sentence begins."

Vertical line: the sign of life, health, activity, certainty, effective stability, manliness. It is the symbol of spirit directed upward, of grandeur and loftiness, and of man running erect; it is the sign of right and might (staff of justice, scepter, marshal's baton).

Horizontal line: the polar opposite of the vertical, and symbol of the earth, the passive, woman, death, and rest; the material and the earthbound.

Diagonal climbing line: the active will to ascend, to develop, to progress. It misses the stability, rest, and certainty of the vertical and horizontal lines.

Diagonal descending line: line of descent, weakness, decay, slipping off, passivity, and uncertainty.

Cross: one of the oldest and most universal signs, uniting the polar contrasts of vertical and horizontal, of God and the world, of the spiritual and the material, of life and death, of man and woman. It indicates the four points of the compass and the point of intersection: a symbol of what is godlike. After the Crucifixion it became a holy symbol in Christianity and was used in many variations.

St. Andrew's cross: named after the cross on which Saint Andrew died; the Roman border cross also had this form. A connecting symbol and the sign of multiplication.

Tau or hammer cross: the cross on which the Romans nailed their condemned. The sign for balance (weighing scales) and, as the hammer symbol, for right and law (judge's gavel).

Corner sign: shows direction.

Two opposite hook signs united: indicates inner unity, marriage, and spiritual union.

Fork cross: symbolizes men standing with arms raised. Sign of the Trinity and of the path of life divided between good and evil; sign for becoming, being, and decaying.

54

Circle: together with the square and the triangle, the primeval signs. Alike on all sides and the only geometric figure formed with one line with no beginning or end, it is a sign of infinity, eternity, perfection, and God. As a round form it is likewise a symbol of the sun, the cosmos, the earth, and the planets. As a pure form it is a sign of purity; as an embracing sign, a symbol of community ("circle" of family and friends).

Circle with center point: symbol of consummated fertilization, the growing child in the mother's womb; likewise, of the sun in astronomy and astrology and of God's all-seeing eye.

Vertically divided circle: union of the circle and the vertical and as such a symbol of mankind's passion to create. It is also a sign of discord and dissension, particularly when one side is black (division of light and dark).

Horizontally divided circle: more passive, resting womanlike in protecting surroundings; when the lower half is black, it is also a sign of the deed of creation, the division of dry land and water.

Wheel cross: a much-used sign with many meanings—all life as the combination of male and female elements, action and rest, life and death, and earth and cosmos. It symbolizes godlike power, which fulfils the world and preserves all life. It is an old symbol of the sun.

Wheel cross: variation of the preceding sign representing its dynamic character as the driving force of the wheel of time.

Wheel cross: combination of the two preceding crosses, with the character and meaning of both; it contains the Christ symbol when the horizontal line is omitted.

Fish-bladder sign: comes from allowing the much-used S-line to divide a circle so that both form one harmonious whole. It is the basis of the famous Chinese yang-yin sign symbolizing perfect antithesis (fig. 5-3).

Pinwheel: two S-lines crossing each other, creating movement; a very harmonious sign.

Pinwheel: four S-lines crossing one another is a sign of restless industry and creative work; also used as a sun wheel. Another variation using eight S-lines is used a great deal in folk art.

Two half-circles: separated from each other, these symbolize the maturing and aging man, the eternal coming and going, ebb and flow, day and night, summer and winter.

Spiral: indicates that all life develops from one point and, still spinning from that one point, grows to adulthood. Also a symbol of the rising sun and the year. Much loved as an ornamental sign in many variations and combinations in all times and by all peoples.

Double spiral: the magnificent sign for perfection—in fact, a completed S-line. Symbol of the day between the rising and the setting sun and leap year (since a single spiral represents one year).

Figure eight: the loop without end and therefore symbolic of endless, eternal time, which has no beginning or end.

Square: one of the three basic signs. Symbol of massiveness, sturdy peace, and stability: it stands fast and firm on the ground. It is the same on all sides and the token for the number four, therefore, it symbolizes the four seasons, the four points of the compass, the four elements, the four rivers of Paradise, and the four Evangelists.

Cross in square: the horizontal and vertical lines divide the square into four similar smaller squares; the cross strengthens the stability of the sign.

Diagonal in square (or fire eye): the symbol of earth, formed and held together by the four elements, earth, water, fire, and light. Sign of life— the power of growth and increase.

Cross and diagonal in square: a strong ornamental effect is derived from fitting both sets dividing lines in the square—its great strength and massiveness are broken down. The eight equal-sided triangles are a sign of the many activities of mankind.

Diamond in square: the diamond is the ancient symbol of the power of creation, the life-bearing womb, granted to woman by God; here protected by the male square sign.

Overlapping of two squares: the ordered and restful character of the square has disappeared, the sign is disturbed; in place of the clear and simple is confusion and uncertainty.

Triangle: the third of the basic, primary signs. It is an aggressive sign with its points directed outwards. It is the symbol of the Trinity and, with a point in the middle, a sign of the all-seeing eye of God. A triangle standing with its base firmly planted on the ground and its point striving upwards has a womanly character, as opposed to a triangle balanced on its point with broad "shoulders" above, which has a more manly character.

Hourglass: both triangles move towards each other, their points touch, and a new figure is created with a new significance, without losing the value of the triangles.

Bisected diamond: the triangles here have a common base. They have become a diamond, in which the upward and downward points indicate an active verticality.

Triangle in circle: signifies the powers that lie dormant in every living being. It is a sign of the unity in the Trinity; with a point in the middle it represents the power of Mary.

Hexagram: two triangles passing through each other create a new sign, a beautiful symmetrical star. It is a magic sign of preservation and protection against destruction; also a very old Jewish sign, the Star of David, that crowns the synagogue and decorates the Torah rolls, as well as an emblem of the cosmos, the divine Creator, and His work.

Pentacle: another very old sign, known as the druid's foot for its magical meaning. Pointing upwards, it is a symbol of white magic; downwards, of black magic. This sign shows the five senses and indicates the powers and forms in nature. The lines intersect one another in golden-section proportions.

Septagram: a sign of cooperation, representing the seven forces of the world. Like the pentagram, it is a protecting sign and is put on doors, gates, toolboxes, etc. When the point is facing downwards, it is a sign of the unholy and means discontent and trouble. In popular speech it was called "the angry seven."

Nonagram: consists of three equilateral triangles placed over one another. It was a sign for the magic numbers three and nine.

Fig. 5-1.

Fig. 5-2.

Fig. 5-3. The symbol of Chinese universalism, with the famous yang-yin symbol in the center. Yin signifies womanly, dark, bound to the earth, cool, reticent, oppressed; yang, manly, light, heavenly, aggressive, warm, governing. The white dot in the dark yin and the dark dot in the light yang signifies that each is always a part of the other. The yang-yin symbol is surrounded by eight Chinese trigrams. Beginning at the top, middle and turning clockwise, their meanings are *kien,* strong, heavenly, father; *sun,* soft, wind, first daughter; *li,* lasting, radiant, fire, second daughter; *tchen,* causal, active, thunder, first son; *kun,* earth, mother, giving; *ken,* hold still, resting, mountain, third son; *kan,* dangerous, water, second son; *tui,* happy, animated, ocean, third daughter.

Cool, moist and passive

58

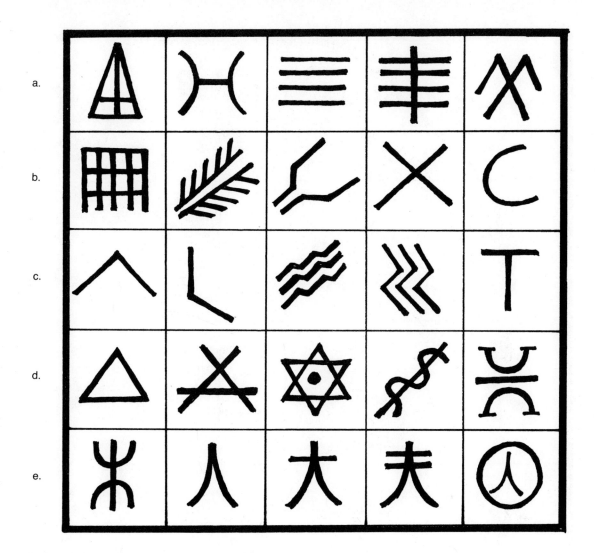

Fig. 5-4. Signs and symbols from different cultures. (a.) Old Eastern: king, life between waxing and waning moon, four world zones or four elements, soul climbs through four world spheres to purification, mountains; (b.) Old Eastern: fishnet, splitting, spreading, protecting, bow; (c.) Assyrian: lie, oppress, water, light, balance; (d.) Negro: active spirit, disturbed spirit, fiery love, true and false witness before a judge, separation or quarrel between man and woman; (e.) Chinese: tree, human being, great, god or heaven, imprisoned.

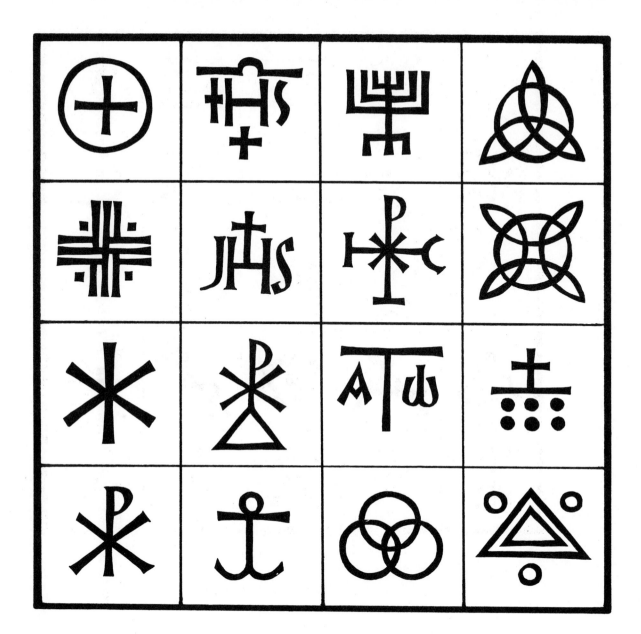

Fig. 5-5. Some of the best-known Christian symbols, selected from the *Book of Signs* by Rudolf Koch. From left to right, beginning top left: cross for the consecration of a church building; monogram of Jesus with the old sign of the Holy Ghost above it; menorah, the seven-branched candleholder, symbol of the Old Testament; sign used for driving out angry spirits; Roman consecration cross; Jesus monogram; connecting symbol of the Christ monogram with the letters *I* and *C* (Greek *S*), meaning Jesus Savior; sign used to drive out angry spirits; the most widespread and oldest Christ monogram; symbol of the Trinity; the Tau cross with the Alpha and Omega; the earth (grains of sand), on which the cross is erected; the labarum, Constantine's standard bearing the monogram of Christ; Christ, the anchor, the hope of the Christians; sign of the Trinity; sign of the Trinity.

Fig. 5-6. More common Christian symbols. From left to right, beginning top left: the all-seeing eye of God; the fish, ichthus, letters of the name Christus; the fish, Christ, beginning and end; the fish, bread and wine (Eucharist); the fish, Christ, in the form of bread and wine (Eucharist); the fish and basket with bread; sign of the miracle of the loaves and fishes; butterfly (and bird), symbol of the soaring soul of mankind; the ship of life on its way to the heavenly harbor; the peacock, symbol of the immortal; the dove as a symbol of the Holy Spirit; the dove as a symbol of purity; the phoenix as a symbol of the resurrection of Christ; the lamb (Christ as slain innocent) with the cross of victory on the book with the seven seals; the eagle (the Holy Ghost) grasps the fish (the Christians) out of the bitter sea of life to bring it to the Light; "As the deer longs for the spring, so my soul yearns for you, oh Lord!" (Bible).

Fig. 5-7. Variations on the cross motif: two primeval signs, the vertical and horizontal, united in one sign. The cross was already in use as an ornament and mystic sign before the death of Christ. It has been used as a decorative motif in all ages, by all peoples, and in all techniques; it is also hidden in the elementary figures (square, circle, diamond). The following well-known crosses are shown here: Jerusalem (a., b., c.), swastika (e.), heraldic cross (f.), Maltese cross (j.), flower cross (l.), fleur-de-lys cross (r.), Huguenot cross (s.), Russian cross (t.), Celtic cross (w.), anchor cross (x.), Christ monogram or Constantine cross (y.).

62

Fig. 5-8. Ornamentations with symbolic meanings. For many primitive peoples these are still living signs rather than mere ornaments. (a.) up and down, sun, water, breathing; (b.) changing of day and night; (c.) between day and night, a middle zone (Spice Islands); (d.) triangles with shading, ebb and flow; (e.) sun, alternating between morning horizon and zenith (Philippines); (f.) cross in daylight (Borneo); (g.) rhythm of water; (h.) ebb and flow (Congo); (i.) sun above and below water (Pueblo Indian); (j.) water in the form of breasts; (k.) eternal passage of the years; (l.) changing moon in the north; (m.) changing moon in the south; (n.) succession of dark moons; (o.) succession of light moons (Celebes); (p., q., r., s., t.) continuous sun years (Fiji Islands).

PART III. ORNAMENTS

6. A New Awakening

"Ornamentation" has been a suspect word for years among architects', designers', and art critics' circles, but that time has passed. Now, when we look around us, everything in sight is color and ornament. Color in interiors, in fashion, in printing—journals, packaging, labels. Ornament in sculpture, on furniture, on curtains and drapes, on the body, on wrapping papers, boxes, bags, and plastic foil!

The prediction made by the Viennese architect Adolf Loos in 1910 that ornamentation had been swept away for good has turned out very differently. In the same year Kandinsky made the remarkable prophecy: "At the end of our present-day twilight period, there might well develop a whole new ornamentation."

Through the work of Kandinsky, Klee, Matisse, Herbin, Picasso, Vasarely, and the Op and Pop artists Hundertwasser, Alt, Bubenik, Capogrossi, Stella, and others, color and ornament have taken possession of our world, and young people have grasped this trend with both hands. Many factors have opened the sluicegates of color and ornament—hobbies, do-it-yourself projects for the home and clothing, community-type houses.

For this reason I have reassembled the fundamentals of decoration, ornamentation, and decor with the intention of showing how they can be used in a responsible manner so that the results will be pleasing and will lead to further experimentation.

In every man there is a certain inborn creative ability and a need for cadence and rhythm, which expresses itself in dancing, singing, and movement and also in ornamentation—which is closely allied to these. Throughout history mankind has had this need, as is quite evident from the range of drawings in this book. At the same time it will become evident that the most beautiful and the strongest ornaments, in spite of the differences in styles in different periods, have all developed from the same basic patterns. In the course of centuries man has developed hundreds of thousands of variations on these simple, basic forms.

I have selected the illustrations in this book with great care in order to give a good picture of the richness and variety of ornamentation created by all peoples in all times. Designs should not be constructed with ruler and compass but rather organically, freehand with whatever tool is appropriate to the occasion. The field of ornamentation is very extensive: it embraces many interesting problems, one of which is the question whether we should apply it to mechanically manufactured products, and if so, how it should compare with the old ornamentation, the ornamentation of "primitive" peoples, the ornamentation in arts and crafts and folk art.

The drawings and illustrations are not intended as examples but only as an incentive to seek contemporary variations and possibilities.

7. Early Ornamentation

Ornamentation is one of the oldest expressions of human creativity, beginning with decoration of the body; pressing on or scratching in burls, stripes, and other elementary forms in pottery; and decoration of coats of arms, small articles, materials, and buildings.

The ornamentation itself can form an organic and logical part of the object, emphasize certain places or parts and increase their value, or detract the eye from them. But if it is not done well, it can damage and obscure the form and, by overloading it, even destroy it entirely.

The language of form in ornamentation hovers between abstract geometry and modes of expression based on nature, from the simplest border of dots or stripes to the very complex animal ornamentation of the Celts and Vikings and the dynamic scroll forms of the Rococo period. Based on the unchangeable fundamentals, every period of culture has developed its own treasure chest of ornamentation.

The basic motifs of ornamentation have appeared in thousands of variations on pottery and other articles since prehistoric times.

The Bronze and Ice Ages used circle, spiral, and meander motifs; in Egypt the lotus was very popular, and the great buildings of the Land of Two Rivers (Babylon) were decorated with magnificent animal figures and borders with palms and rosettes, all executed in colorful ceramics. In the reliefs of the Persians, Hittites, and other peoples of the Middle East animals, human figures, and plants were combined in a splendid ornamental and monumental unity. The Greeks, Romans, and Etruscans accented their edifices, vases, and implements with geometric decorations and ornamentation borrowed from nature, often superbly integrated into the forms (palmettes, acanthus leaves, shoots, etc.).

In contrast to classical ornamentation, a whole new style of ornament developed in the North, characterized by a frequently complicated string of animal and vegetation borders.

By virtue of its inner strength and simplicity, the ornamentation of the early Middle Ages must be regarded as outstanding.

The development of Ottoman ornament in the great mosques in Persia and the Middle East must also be regarded highly. In spite of the Koran's prohibition on the use of animal and human figures, these works of art bear witness to a high culture. The masterpieces in the Far East such as the Angkor Wat temple, the reliefs of the Boro-Bodur of Java, and the magnificent examples of ornamental art in the Indochinese Khmer kingdoms—only just discovered in this century—give us a picture of admirable accomplishment.

68

This estimation applies no less to the abundant, decorative temple art in India, where many old cultures have left their traces. Ornamental artists in China exercised their richest fantasy and greatest ability on bronzes. The old temple cities of the Mayas in Yucatan and Honduras and of the other great American cultures reveal such a treasure of ornamental forms of decoration, both geometric and natural, that we wonder how they came into being.

The Gothic period introduced a geometric interplay within the shapes of windows, rose windows, and other expanses of the cathedral walls.

The Renaissance, Baroque, and Rococo periods used ornamentation with such superabundance and complicated inventiveness in architecture and on clothing, furniture, utensils, and purely decorative articles that its subordinate, complementary function was often totally negated.

Biedermeyer and the Empire period stemmed this tradition in Western Europe, and classicism restored the old forms once again, but bloodlessness and aridity are characteristic of the period.

Around 1900, ornamentation became the object of heated discussion and was maligned under the leadership of the Viennese architect Adolf Loos ("Ornament is a crime ") and the artists of the new functionalism, for whom function and beauty were one and the same and lack of decoration an ideal. The Youth Style, also known as the Vermicelli style, reacted with a return to naturalistic ornamentation.

The desire for decoration and adornment is so strongly inbred in man that nowadays he wants it on industrial products as well. The youth of today have made color and ornamentation an integral part of their lives.

Order and Variation in Elementary Ornamentation

It is always difficult to try to classify and rank the creative works of man in terms of categories and importance. The case of ornamentation, with its endless possibilities of variation, proved no different.

The following synopsis, which is based on the analysis devised by Wolfgang von Wersin, restricts itself to basic forms, i.e., rhythmic, simple ornamentation, adapted and developed by all peoples in all ages and in all parts of the world. It is a sort of universal handwriting of mankind: it is as inborn as dancing, cadence, and rhythm. It flows by itself, as it were, playfully from his hands and, according to his character and the circumstances, appears as a softly undulating line, an angular, hard, zigzag line, the introspective line of a circle, or one of many other designs.

This outline contains in essence all the possibilities of the elementary patterns, and all rhythmic ornamentation can be categorized in this outline. Each of the basic forms can be varied in a thousand different ways. The outline is in fact a triptych.

1. The two left-hand panels show patterns of separated elements, the left with lines, the right with spotlike elements.

2. The two middle panels show patterns of contrasting elements, again, the left linear and the right spotlike.

3. The two right-hand panels show patterns of interlacing elements, again, the left linear, the right spotlike.

The top row of six panels gives the most elementary form of each pattern: in each panel the ornament is used as a border or band and as a continuous design on a plane.

Fig. 7-1.

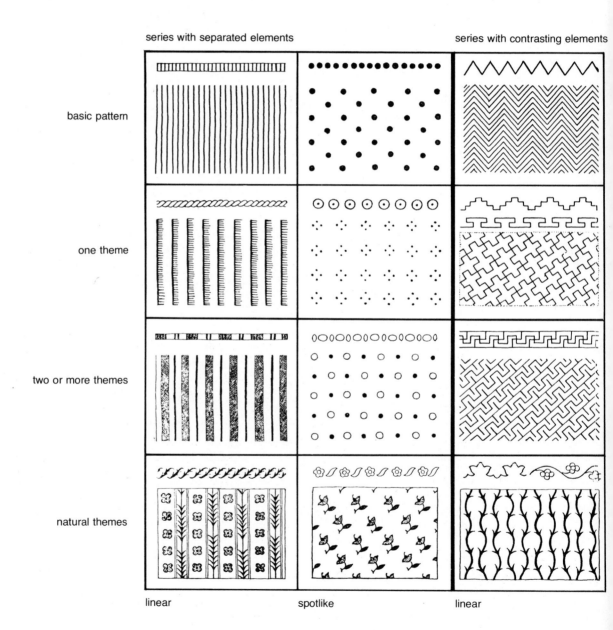

series with separated elements

series with contrasting elements

basic pattern

one theme

two or more themes

natural themes

linear

spotlike

linear

70

The second row is the first variation: the single line of the basic form has become a more complex element, still, however, alike, the same theme.

The third row modifies the second into thin and thick lines or bands, rhythmically placed next to each other. There are now two themes, which can be extended indefinitely.

The bottom row has the same abstract structure as the third row but uses forms borrowed from nature, again as a border and as a plane.

series with overlapping elements

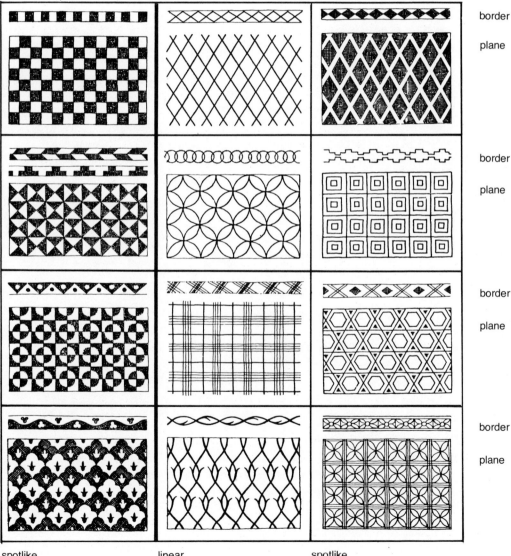

border

plane

border

plane

border

plane

border

plane

spotlike   linear   spotlike

The outline clearly shows once again that the very existence of ornament is based on play between contrasts: stillness and movement, horizontal and vertical, thick and thin, round and angular. It may be one of the proofs for the fact that making ornamentation is one of the primeval talents of mankind and that it finds its origin in all the events and things that accompany him like strange contradictions on his path through life.

To avoid excessive and pointless decoration, to find the way back to simple and expressive power—this remains the stamp of true ornament. The following points show the way:

1. Ornament is rhythm made visible, whether arranged as a band or border or spread over a plane.

2. Ornament can be adapted both to a flat plane (regular or less regular figures) and to spatial forms, either simple or composite (architecture).

3. Ornament can be created by means of geometrical motifs and by motifs borrowed from nature.

4. Ornamentation is in essence an abstract form of expression, like music and dance, and it emanates from the deeper regions of human nature.

5. Ornamentation lies in the very being of mankind and is, like all art, universal.

6. Ornamentation is bound by strict rules of moderation: rhythm, form, material, and technique.

7. Ornament must be subservient to the article itself.

8. All ornamentation must begin at the beginning. The beginning is a given plane or given form, not the motif, however interesting it might be: first rhythm and then motif.

9. The design of an ornament for a plane divides that plane: the division is organic, it arises by itself out of the plane.

10. To ornament is to accentuate meaning. It must be used sparingly, never where it serves no purpose or is superfluous. Do not use stylized forms, forms distorted from nature, or historical-style forms.

The Earliest Ornamental Forms of Mankind

Ornamentation is a language of signs, which come from the deeper regions of human nature where mimicry, gesture, song, and dance originate.

The spontaneous emotions of human nature seek ever more confined forms. These confined, yet visible forms find expression in the life powers present in the human body and in the whole of nature: the bifurcation of breath and the beat of the heart; the alternation of day and night, of light and dark; the rhythm of the seasons; rise and fall, ebb and flow.

The rhythmic course of all life forces in creation, with their up-and-down or to-and-fro movement, is the same force from which true, living ornamentation has always been derived.

Scholars have not yet agreed on the origin of ornamentation. It is generally assumed that its beginning must be sought in the need to adorn the human body and that magical reasons as well as the simple desire to decorate the body were present. A difference of opinion arises over the remarkable difference between naturalistic and geometric ornamentation; itinerant huntsmen expressed themselves in naturalistic imagery and ornament, while later indigenous agricultural peoples used abstract, geometric forms. Fig. 7-2 illustrates both forms.

Fig. 7-2.

Fig. 7-2a is an example of one of the oldest forms of ornament, a bead necklace, made here from the larger teeth of a red deer, trout vertebrae, and small seashells strung together in a beautiful, rhythmic pattern. It could easily have been made today, and yet this necklace, completely intact just as it is illustrated here, was found along with several others in a grave at Menton on the Riviera. The grave contained the skeleton of a full-grown man, a younger woman, and a child of about fifteen years, and it is dated at about 10,000 to 15,000 years before recorded time.

Fig. 7-2b is a so-called commando staff made from a piece of reindeer horn and engraved with naturalistic wild horses. Equally naturalistic are the engravings on pieces of bone found in the Swiss grottoes (fig. 7-2f). The purpose of the commando staffs is not known, although it is assumed that they played some role in hunting.

All the other illustrations are examples of the geometric style. The decorated pebbles, of which many hundreds have been found in different places, can be divided into three groups: the so-called counting stones (fig. 7-2c), with vertical stripes or dots; the stones with graphic or symbolic significance (figs. 7-2d and e); and the letter stones, which strongly resemble our own letter signs (fig. 7-2e, bottom left, looks like e or m). Whatever their explanation, the letter stones were certainly not the instruction media of a prehistoric village school!

Fig. 7-2g shows a simple zigzag ornament and a very ingenious meander design; both are evidence that there is nothing new under the sun, since they were carved on a mammoth's tooth 10,000 years B.C. as armband decorations.

Fig. 7-2h is a fully schematized female nude engraved on ivory. It dates from the European Middle Stone Age.

It seems to me highly dangerous to try to "explain" these pictorial forms in scientific terms. All of these designs are very strong and fundamental ornamental forms, which proves to me personally that ornamentation is inherent in human nature and dependent on neither time nor place.

Are there not, moreover, other phenomena in nature that defy scientific explanation? I name but a few examples. What deeper forces control the secret flight of migrating birds? Is this order their own symbol sign, or is it merely a functional streamline to reduce air resistance? What is the deeper meaning of the secret battle order of the soldier ants or the dance flight of the terns? Does the yearning for decoration and ornamentation only begin with man?

Fig. 7-4. Bell beaker found in the Veluwe region and dating from 1800–1500 B.C. This type spread all over Europe at the end of the Stone Age. This ornament, consisting of scratched in, geometric forms, is divided into three zones. The ornament on the neck consists of stripes and bands of different motifs, with a rich finish on the rim. The shoulder of the pot is divided into panels, alternately without decoration and with an attractive diagonal filling. The decoration of this bell beaker, rhythmically and sensitively distributed over the surface, rivals the Greek vase shown in fig. 7-5b, which was not scratched in but painted. (Collection of the State Museum of Antiquities, Leiden.)

◀

Fig. 7-3. This magnificent large beaker, over a foot tall, was found near Stroe in the Veluwe region. It dates from 2000 B.C. and was made by an artist who possessed not only the skill to build up such a large pot from rolls of clay and a well-developed sense of shape (see the tension in the silhouette line) but also desire, patience, dedication, and feeling for decoration. Alternating bands around the body of the vase, sometimes three lines, sometimes plastic squares with a rounded-off surface, make it a masterpiece of prehistoric work. (Photo by Dienst Rijksoudheidkundig Bodemonderzoek.)

Fig. 7-5.

a.

b.

c.

d.

78

Geometric Motifs on Old Ceramics

One of the most beautiful examples of geometric ornamentation is a thin-walled beaker of white clay from Susa dated 4000 to 3000 B.C. (fig. 7-5a). The ornamental division is particularly beautiful: a dark foot, then three horizontal white lines. The upper section is divided by vertical lines that contrast with the main motif, a goat, whose enormous horns form a strong circle. Inside this is another motif, a geometric plant design; the rump of the goat is integrated into the circle motif. The border above is formed by a sort of long, low dachshund, which gives the effect of a horizontal line with a playful unevenness. One broad and several narrow horizontal lines form the division between this border and the border frieze above, which consists of a fine row of what appear to be vertical lines but are in fact the long necks of cranes, whose beaks and bodies create a particularly sensitive embellishment. This magnificent old beaker is one of the highlights of ornamental art, adapting animal forms with great conviction and mastery as living and monumental ornamentation. It can only be compared with certain expressions of Oceanic ornamental art.

Other highlights of the geometric style of ornamentation are shown in the two Greek vases (figs. 7-5b and c). They exhibit a rich pattern of horizontally running bands in which a number of motifs offset one another in a fine rhythm: zigzag and undulating lines, dots, triangles, diamonds, circles, and, above all, striking meander borders. There is a well-balanced division between base and decoration in each piece, and everything stands exactly in its place. Fig. 7-5b has only geometric variations, whereas fig. 7-5c, the large vase from Dipylon, near Athens, illustrates a tendency to use animal and human figures in borders. The neck of the vase (used for storage or sacrificial purposes) shows a vertical ornament with a horizontal meander border above and below it. The shoulder of the vase is decorated with animal figures (including horses, bulls, ibex, wild boar, deer, lions, panthers, and sphinxes). The dominant main border is formed by the complex meander followed by a border of diamonds and a narrow band of aquatic birds. Dipylon vases have exhausted every possibility of the geometric style of ornamentation.

The Pueblo Indian field bottle (figure 7-5d) is completely decorated with geometric designs.

Fig. 7-7. Cylinder-shaped beaker from the pre-Columbian Nazca-Huari culture (circa 600–500 B.C.). It consists of a black diamond pattern on a white background; the filled-in color is a reddish-brown. Symbolic motifs with a freer line top off the strict geometric pattern in a particularly sensitive way. (Collection of Dr. J. F. da Costa.)

Fig. 7-6. Attic earthenware jug, dating from the 8th century B.C. This jug is a typical example of the Dipylon style (the name comes from the churchyard by the city wall of Athens where a great quantity of these jugs were found). It is about seventeen inches tall. The ornamentation shows a magnificent variety of geometric motifs. The main band around the belly consists of panels filled in with diamond shapes; the shoulders, of a transitional motif running from the neck to the body; the underside, of fine lines; and the neck, of a large meander motif. (Collection of the State Museum of Antiquities, Leiden.)

80

Fig. 7-8. Twisted bronze neck ring found in the Veluwe region. This neck ring, dating from 700–500 B.C., shows the high quality of workmanship of the early Hallstatt culture in Central Europe. It was presumably used as an offering. The plastic effect of the double twist (twisted in a molten state) is particularly beautiful. (Collection of the State Museum of Antiquities, Leiden.)

old ceramic

Molukken

Molukken

Moluccas

Moluccas

Philippines

Philippines (Celebes)

Borneo

China

Congo

New Zealand

South Africa

Congo (Kassai)

Carolines

Ceylon

Siberia

Tibet

Dahomey

Borneo

New Guinea

Eskimo

California Indian

Pueblo Indian

Peru

Peru

Central Brazil

Fig. 7-9. The zigzag motif in a few of its thousands of variations. As this page shows, it has been adapted by all peoples of the world, from prehistoric times to the present day. It is one of the universal signs that mankind has developed.

Fig. 7-10. Prints of cylindrical and flat seals and stamps from Mexico. Early American civilizations, which exhibited great differences among themselves, reveal fascinating contrasts to what happened in the Old World. The most important cultures are the Aztecs in Mexico, the Mayas in Yucatan and Guatemala, and the Incas in Peru (all between 500–1500 A.D.). These illustrations show the strongly decorative ornamentation of the Aztecs, who were masters in earthenware. (a., b.) geometric motifs; (c., d.) squares with ornamental crosses; (e.) seal with man's head; (f.) flat stamp representing a panther; (g.) round seal with human figure; (h.) rectangular stamp with ape motif; (i.) stamp with deer; (j.) fish motif; (k.) bird; (l.) spiral motif; (m.) double spiral.

Fig. 7-11. Round ornamental motifs from pre-Columbian Mexico. They utilize many different designs: geometric, flowers, animals, and human figures, all of them excellently adapted to the round shape.

82

Fig. 7-12. Among the most beautiful examples of symbolic ornamental art are the famous Gothic picture stones found in Sweden. These stones, dating from circa 500 B.C., were not grave monuments but part of a sun cult, and they were placed on high, special locations. The principal image of the stone of Vall-stena illustrated here is a spiral sun symbol surrounded by five smaller sun signs, with two men fighting below and two animals above. The stones themselves are in the form of an ax, and the representations are laid out in a magnificent, straight, low relief. (Drawing by Ulli Winkler.)

Fig. 7-13. Examples of Viking art, which was characterized by the integration of band-and-plaiting ornamentation and bandlike animal figures into a complicated whole. From left to right: dragon's head carved from wood from the infamous Oseberg ship; two bronze buckles; an ornamental lid of a wooden box with notching; lid of the Cordula shrine from the cathedral treasure of Cammin, carved from walrus bone and, along with the other sides, mounted in bronze.

8. Geometry & Ornamentation

People of all times and cultures have been stimulated and inspired by the elementary signs, especially the circle, square, and triangle. A normal, healthy man senses these three basic figures intuitively, because they lie concealed in his spirit and his whole being. They are the clearest and simplest forms, basically very different from one another in spite of their inner relationship.

What is the cause of the powerful expressiveness of these age-old forms? In his subconscious, every man is pervaded by the conviction that behind the whole of creation there is a strict order, a compelling law of regulation. He experiences it in the course of the heavenly bodies, in the succession of the seasons, in life and death, in thunder and lightning, in the growth of plants.

The human eye and sensibility is gratified whenever man finds orderly construction in a work of art: the power, simplicity, and direct expressiveness of the basic forms. The forms give him calm and reassurance.

The three fundamental signs are clear and simple and at the same time secretive and evasive. They bear a clear relationship to one another in spite of their opposing expressions. The figures invite one to a game that is stimulating and inexhaustible. They evoke, as if by themselves, imaginary lines, which are a part of their being and which the eye discovers without hesitation.

The illustrations in this chapter show some of the results of this game, which everyone can try for himself in his own way and according to his own character, inasmuch as the possibilities are limitless.

There is an unmistakable relationship between geometry and beauty. The regimentation, precariousness, and moderation of these forms open our eyes to the geometric game by which nature constructs and endlessly varies itself.

The three basic forms, whether they be two- or three-dimensional (sphere, cube, or pyramid), have always awakened in man a feeling of seriousness, greatness, and monumentality.

The fundamental forms lay the foundations of many large constructions in one way or another. They form the beginning and the end for today's designer.

The fascination of the fundamental figures and forms was expressed by Goethe in *Faust* as follows:

How different is this sign affecting me!
I can see in these pure lines
Active nature lying before my soul . . .
How everything weaves to a whole!
One acts and lives in the other!

Paul Klee has said that three worlds express themselves in the three fundamental forms:

1. The square expresses the world of the heavy, the fixed (the earth).

2. The circle expresses the spiritual world of the feelings, movement, the ethereal (water).

3. The triangle expresses the intellectual world of logic, the concentration of light and fire.

Drawing Exercises with the Primary Figures

Visual communication has become important in our time through publicity, advertisement, graphics, design, and other similar fields. The picture has become so important in interhuman relations that all teaching, not only teaching in art, has been affected by it.

Fig. 8-1. These figures are the symbols of cleanliness, power, clarity, and evenness; they are the fundamental figures, the beginning and end of all form. Their spatial equivalents are the cube, sphere, and equilateral pyramid. The expressive power of these figures, which are so different and yet have such close mathematical relationships, has inspired many to speak of the "dynamic beauty of geometric forms." What the Greeks found in their geometry is still valid, unabridged, and unchanged, especially now when so many artists feel a need to strip art of the excessively personal.

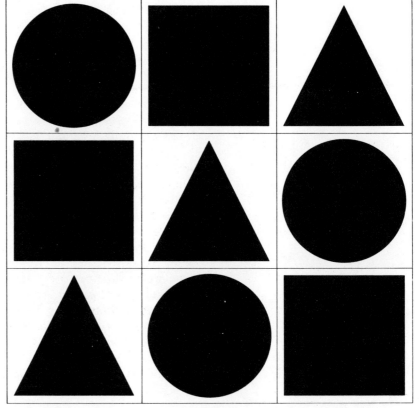

Visual communication makes use of modern aids and appliances and will do so much more in the future, since such techniques and sciences at our disposal as thinking and designing computers and letter and sign systems help worldwide communication. Teaching machines will very soon lighten the load of the teacher. Already many large industries are engaged in the development of the hardware (apparatus) and software (teaching material, systems, programs, etc.) that will eventually commit to tape all the knowledge and learning of mankind.

In teaching art design it is important that, in addition to exercises in free expression, attention be paid to the constructive language of geometry by means of exercises and experiments with the primary figures: square, triangle, and circle.

I have always been fascinated by the power and the secret of the primary figures and bodies in geometry, by numbers and number relationships, and by their connection with the structure of earth and space. Moreover, I am of the opinion that the primary forms are so strongly embedded in the subconscious of every designer that they must inevitably have been the starting point of all thought on form.

My art-design classes always begin by introducing the concepts of point, line, space, size, number, rhythm, proportion—all the concepts that are involved with the creation of form. I start with the apparently easy game of playing with the square—its possibilities, variable divisions, and combinations with the other primary figures. This is done in many different media: nature study, color exercises, technical drawing, and spatial experiments with clay, plaster, wood, paper, and cardboard.

The object of the exercises with the primary figures is the following:

1. To examine and analyze these regular forms.

2. To get to know the character of each of these forms by studying the lines and divisions that seem to spring from the forms themselves.

3. To discover the rich possibilities within these simplest forms and at the same time to discover that the most direct, most obvious, most simple divisions are the most beautiful and the most harmonious.

4. To assemble pages of variations, which not only form a unity but at the same time are clearly distinct from one another.

5. To cultivate a love and a desire for order and regulation, for clarity and cleanliness, for painstaking work.

6. To stimulate imagination, feeling for logic, exercise of the eye, and, above all, insight into the creative process through intensive occupation with these tasks.

In all my classes I have found that every one of my students without exception worked on these projects with a great deal of animation and pleasure. Furthermore, all the students, even the less gifted ones, could bring this sort of exercise to a satisfactory conclusion.

In spite of the concrete limitations of the projects—sometimes they were done in black and white, sometimes in color; sometimes freehand, sometimes with drafting tools—it seemed again and again that every page had its own character and that there was no uniformity. The students never expressed the opinion that they felt themselves restricted by too narrow a range of choice.

Some of these exercises are shown in figs. 8-2–8-8. They were done on graph paper of varying scales. Additional applications of geometry to ornamentation are shown in figs. 8-9–8-17.

Fig. 8-2. Variations of dividing the square by horizontal and vertical lines. The lower-right-hand illustration shows seven strips of white paper arranged to obtain a logical and pleasing composition with an ornamental character.

Fig. 8-3. Possibilities and variations of diagonals within the square. The diagonal divisions reveal a totally different character from the horizontal/vertical lines.

Fig. 8-4. This figure shows a number of variations on the circle (or segments) in the square, combined or not with both of the preceding exercises. The possibilities of variation within these three elementary figures are endless, even without any use of color.

Fig. 8-5. (a.) Variations based on the pentagon and hexagon within the circle. These forms and divisions appear many times in nature (flowers, snow crystals, bisections of stems and organs). (b.) Ornamental games based on the equilateral triangle within the circle.

Figs. 8-6 and 8-7. These figures illustrate how unlimited patterns can be created by placing simple elements next to one another in a given network (here, a checkerboard). Through simple repetition of one and the same motif logical and organic ornamentation can be produced.

90

Fig. 8–7.

Fig. 8-8. Draw a large square on a sheet of paper and divide it into smaller squares, like a checkerboard. Make a composition, using variations on the three elementary figures to create a good, harmonious division of the plane up and down, across, around, and diagonally. Whether you use colors or black, white, and gray, they should be well distributed over the plane. Try adding one color, e.g., red, to the black, white, and gray. Or use two contrasting colors, which, together with the white, black, and gray, can produce a rich range of harmony: the two pure colors, pure white and black, each color blended with white and black, and each color blended with a range of the grays from light to dark.

Fig. 8-9. Alternating ornament. The network is based on squares, within which are circle borders, themselves containing star forms made with quarter circles (not exact). The figures are then filled in, alternately black and white, which produces the lively and organic effect.

Fig. 8-10. N. J. van de Vecht was the first person in this century to restate the ground rules for ornamentation based on the nature and mathematics of the area to be decorated. The methods popular at that time, which were frequently based on stylizing nature or free art founded on the motif, went by the board with his lucid and convincing exposé. Van de Vecht's ideas seem too mathematical today. Nevertheless, they were influential in sweeping away the rage for stylization. This illustration, reproduced from van de Vecht's first book, shows possibilities that can be developed from the hexagon in the square, e.g., divisions in border and surface springing from the points and lines of the hexagon. The divisions created by this apparently reasonable geometric method are governed by an inner logic, a system of structure, that offers more security than so-called intuitive divisions. Josef Albers' "homage to the square" is a corroboration of this point of view.

Fig. 8-11. This beautiful figure creates itself by joining twenty-four points on the
circumference of the circle. A further
analysis will reveal other geometrical
phenomena.

Fig. 8-12. Four figures by Hermann von Baravalle, showing movement and ornamentation on a circle whose radius is smaller than that of the beginning circle.

Fig. 8-13. Four variations on experiments carried out by Dr. Hans Jenny, whereby vibrations were made visible. His documentation of the structure and dynamics of vibration gives a stimulating insight into the richness and lawfulness of nature and once again illustrates how geometry and ornament are related. The sonorous figures of Chladni (1756–1827), made by vibrating fine sand on a metal plate and stroking it with the bow of a violin, were used for the experiments. The illustrations bear a certain relationship to one another. Their complexity depends upon the frequency of the pitch: above left, a figure created by the lowest frequency; below right, by the highest.

Fig. 8-14. Ornamental effects created by varying divisions of the plane: here, the impression of diverse rows of bricks. Design networks are created in the same way.

Fig. 8-15. Another page from van de Vecht, showing variations on triangles, pentagons, and hexagons. Many contemporary artists (Vasarely, Lhote, Max Bill, etc.) play with form and color movement in their work, which often has a strongly ornamental character, even though the intention and the result extend beyond it.

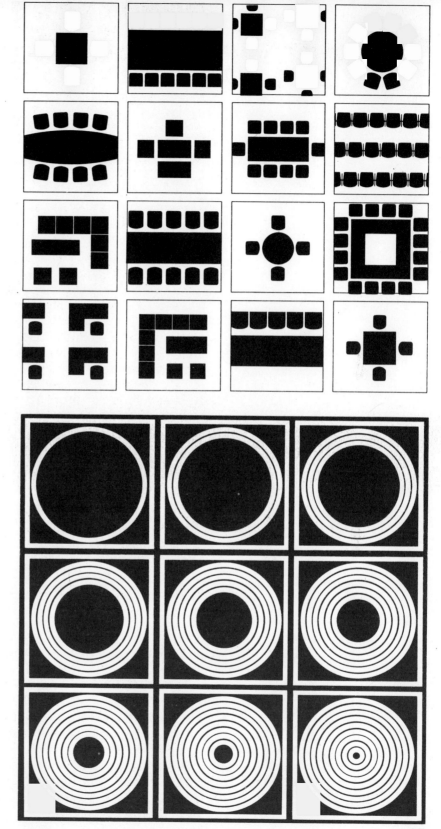

Fig. 8-16. Front page of the Wilkhahn factory furniture catalog, which shows how chairs and tables can be combined.

Fig. 8-17. Graphic designed by Guido Lippens for an invitation to an exhibition. The circle in the square, gradually thickening in nine steps, is an interesting plastic and ornamental problem. The eye can focus on either the black or the white, which constantly evokes new tensions.

9. Ornamentation & Nature

Whenever we think of awe-inspiring and unimaginable cosmic space, the question inevitably arises as to its creation and the powers that have held it in place for billions of years. Now that man, through the enormous development of science and technology, has taken his first, difficult steps into this limitless space and has detached himself from his trusted Mother Earth, we realize more than before that we are not only spectators of a timeless drama of enormous dimensions, in which the acts and intervals last millions of years, but that we, as leading actors, are closely affected by it: that it all revolves around us, and that we too revolve in the eternal cycle of life and death, of rising and setting. Man is unaware, generally speaking, of the greatness and beauty that surrounds him and of the wonder of his own body. The miracle alone of sight—our ability to absorb the niceties of forms, colors, and structures through the construction of our eyes and brains, compared to which all our technology is mere child's play—must give us constant food for thought. It is a great pity that all men possess these powerful instruments but that so few really use them to observe intensively and penetratingly what lies beneath the surface. It is a pity that so little attention is paid in our educational system to teaching children how to observe, for seeing must be learned, and it has nothing to do with complicated theories or instructions. There is no straight, easy path to follow in order to learn to see. We must follow slow, narrow, often hidden paths and sidetracks in order to reach this goal.

Our magnificent world offers an abundance of aids and appliances by means of which we can learn to see. We must therefore be open to the beauties of creation, we must set aside the inhibitions and frustrations that our daily life imposes on us. With the openness of a child we must approach things and absorb them, imprint their images in our thoughts, and carefully store them in that magnificent instrument that is our memory. As Dürer said, "From the treasure of his heart, collected by his eyes, the artist draws his whole life long for the shaping of his ideas." And again, "A good artist is inwardly a full figure, and if it were possible for him to live eternally, then he would, according to the inward ideas of which Plato speaks, always pour out something new in his works."

For the creative man the study of nature is essential. Oscar Schlemmer expressed it this way: "Study nature, take it fully and totally, and then give back the inner face." Paul Klee wrote: "Take your students to Nature, into Nature! Let them experience how a bud forms, how a tree grows, how a butterfly emerges so that they might become just as rich, just as mobile, just as capricious as Mother Nature. Observation is revelation, insight into the workshop of Creation. There lies the secret."

Man himself is a part of creation. He is made up of the same component parts as all life in the cosmos, he obeys the same rules; the proportions of his body are analogous to the rules of proportion in the whole of nature.

It is evident that the spirit of man is pleasurably affected by observation of the order, the purposefulness, the unity in the things of nature, and he finds this harmony beautiful. And he will also find beautiful whatever he creates according to the same rules and regulations.

It is most important that artist and artisan alike study composition in nature. Not to simply copy the forms of nature, as he did in the last century, but to seek the very fundamentals of things, the yardsticks for proportion and harmony, the growth of form and the coherence of form, color, and decoration.

The whole cosmos is built up on a simple scientific canvas that radiates through all forms and all movement. Observe starfish, snow crystals, the mathematically pure spiral of the nautilus, ammonites, the seed pods of fruit, the placing of leaves around stems, cobwebs.

General Concepts

1. Nature, since its primeval beginning, has always spoken but one language; in the first seeds and kernels the laws of composition were laid down and have not changed since.

2. The rules and regulations of composition, size and proportion, and mutual relationships are constant and universal. They lend their validity to the structure and growth of the universe and to the structure of our observations. They are revealed in nature and above all in man himself.

3. Nature creates with economical use of the simplest means a few basic forms and an unending number of variations. The composition of nature is logical in that nothing is ever done arbitrarily. The whole composition of nature is built on the fundamental principle of organic order.

4. Nature works according to the rules of geometry, i.e., it ordains, it creates a certain rhythm; above all it allows a certain elbow room. Rule and elasticity are closely related to one another in nature. That is why it is so many-sided and at the same time so orderly.

5. Since the oldest civilizations man has sought to formulate standards of beauty, and since the beginning man has surmised that in nature a great order and a secret plan of composition ruled, a reflection of which should permeate his own work.

6. Creative man should not just take over or borrow directly from the forms of nature. He must discover its general character and seek no more than simplicity, unity, and harmony; balance, accent, and rhythm. Man is a part of nature, and therefore it is clear that the quintessence of the rules and regulations inherent in nature must also form the quintessence of the rules and regulations inherent in man and his work.

Fig. 9-1.

7. There is no doubt that the engineers of the twentieth century have produced the most important symbols of our time: airplanes, bridges, cranes. Even these machines reveal close relationships to the expressions of organic composition in nature.

8. Through the study of natural forms, the artist and designer must develop to the fullest their feeling for form and proportion; this must seep into their subconscious, and they must intuitively carry it over into their work.

9. The artist must relive the language and inner life of creation in his work.

"Proportion and symmetry are beautiful all over the world!" (Plato).

"When I speak of beauty of form, I mean not the beauty of animals, flowers, paintings but of straight and curved lines, circles, plane and stereometric figures made with compasses and rulers; for I assure you that these possess not only a relative beauty, as do other things, but also an eternal and an absolute beauty" (Socrates).

"The creator has ordained everything according to proportion and number" (Bible).

Symmetry, which in one way or another rules all composition in nature, is based on rules of form that coincide entirely with the laws of geometry. And while geometry constructs figures abstractly, we find in natural figures a living geometry, a free creation based on geometric laws. This is very clearly manifested in the composition of crystals, one of the most beautiful of which is the snow crystal.

If you examine fig. 9-1, you will learn in a very clear and convincing fashion these two important principles of form in nature:

1. All creation, from the infinitely large to the infinitesimally small, is built up and ordered according to set rules and regulations, whose roots lie in mathematics.

2. Nature works with a few basic forms and figures, yet it varies and combines them in an endless and complete manner. Furthermore, nature illustrates here how the essential elements of beauty are based on order, regulation, simplicity, symmetry, balance, alternation, and contrast, rules which aesthetics has also evolved.

Fig. 9-1 shows photographs of crystals, magnified about twenty times. This is only a fraction of the thousands of photographs of snow crystals that have been studied so far, and all of them are different. What is really remarkable, however, is that all are variations on one theme, that there is one dominant and leading factor, the base of these wonderful forms, namely, the hexagon. Water, when crystallized, obeys strict, eternal, and unchanging rules: two parts of hydrogen and one part of oxygen (water is always H_2O) under certain conditions crystallize in a hexagonal system and never any other way! The amazing diversity manifested within this structure is a result of the great variability of different factors: temperature, moisture, air currents in the same cloud, although the general conditions are exactly the same, the crystals differ from one another, yet all belong to the same basic type.

Ornamentation and Structure

A few centuries ago a simple man, Antonie van Leeuwenhoek, saw things that no man before him had ever observed and discovered a world so fascinating, so rich and varied that he thought he was in a dream world. This man's hobby was lenses and lens cutting, and he was the first person to see the movement of blood corpuscles and microbes.

A small world, the microcosmos, had entered the viewing field of man. The small, simple lenses of van Leeuwenhoek have since grown to magnificent optical works of wonder, which embrace the world of creation, the endless space of the universe, and the depth and detail of the infinitely small.

Man examines the smallest component parts of creation and gropes towards the primeval beginnings in order to try to solve the ultimate secrets. Even the world of the small—indeed, here in particular—reveals in a miraculous fashion how everything in creation is based on size and number, on a secret rhythm and a wondrous unit.

A German researcher and an accomplished artist, Ernest Haeckel, saw it as his life's work to commit this fantastic world to paper. He revealed it to mankind in thousands of drawings, one of which is shown in fig. 9-10.

Nature offers to anyone who seeks it a limitless field for the study of structures, which nowadays are used so enthusiastically as ground material for abstract works.

The microscope has opened up new wonders of structure in the world of the minute, and it is evident in the art of today that the beautiful books of microscopic photographs of the beauties of nature have been useful to artists for the recreation of a new, organic ornamentation.

Or should we believe in a miracle, that artists and designers today no longer copy nature but work as nature does, that they have a new insight, and that as a result forms and figures are created that blossom intuitively from creative man because he, himself a part of nature, has opened himself to its rhythm? Many recent works of art have in their drawing, rhythm, and color something that could have been formed and grown in nature itself. This must be regarded as a tremendous gain, as opposed to the tradition of copying the examples set by nature and thinking up all sorts of senseless ornamental frills. We are by no means finished with all that, but we are moving slowly but surely in the right direction.

Impressionism, with its pure colors, and Cubism and Constructivism, with their form, became partners of natural science. Primitive art became a focus of attention because of its strong, expressive power and tectonic construction. Pure forms and clear, functional concepts became the foundation of a new architecture, of modern music, and of a new method of teaching crafts and industrial design.

The famous formula of Cézanne, "Study ball, cone, and cylinder" (for decades men had laughed at this as the hobby of an old, obstinate man), was zealously taken up everywhere. Mondrian and van Doesburg divided the picture plane in horizontals and verticals and used only black and white and the primitive colors (yellow, blue, red) so that, though a rigorous purification, the art of painting might again begin with the purest and simplest means to create in an original, creative way.

Order, proportion, number, lucidity, and clarity became the keystones of a new era.

The microscope revealed a world that formed the scientific proof of all the things that had enthralled and fascinated creative man for centuries. He discovered the world of the diminutive as a playground of elementary forms and powers, of unknown structures and tension fields, of proportion and order: radiolaria, diatoms, cells, and tissues. This wealth of wonder is ruled by square, circle, and triangle, and life here shows its beginning in balls, cubes, cylinders, and cones.

The artist of today who is honestly seeking his most personal form of expression, even if he seems outwardly to use the forms of nature very sparingly, has nevertheless preserved much more of the inner and meaningful conformity to rules than a superficial inspection might reveal.

Moreover, contact with nature gives man a feeling for simplicity and naturalness, and these two things are necessary conditions for man, and in particular for creative man, to reach and further true culture.

Fig. 9-2. Branch tip from an African species of pine. The finer elements grow like basketwork from the thicker stem. The fruits lie like eggs in their decorative nest.

Fig. 9-3. Nerve system of a cordate leaf. The stalk runs as a main artery through the leaf, and the smaller arteries become finer towards the end to form the skeleton. (Photo by Ruth Crevel.)

Fig. 9-4. Root stump of a Mediterranean reed. The growth rings form an accentuating ornament; transitions of shape are particularly emphasized.

Fig. 9-5 (below left). Cross-section of a red cabbage. The packing of leaves yet to grow can be seen here, forming a fascinating linear and ornamental pattern.

Fig. 9-6 (below right). Microphotograph of a preparation from the human brain, another example of the working method of nature: a main stem with side shoots, like rivers, lightning, blood circulation, trees and plants, etc. Man uses the same method when he wants to express organic growth and offshoots, for example, the ornamental plant forms of Matisse.

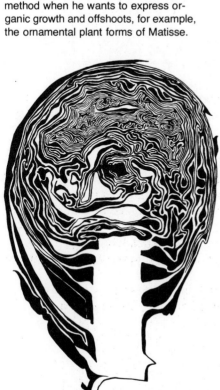

105

Man Recognizes the Creator in the Clothing of Things

"Let us again examine nature and delve into the deepest depths of the oceans and grasp what tension and inner power are there and bring them to the surface—houses and hermitages that swirl in the water, that dance on the waves, that lurch on the breakers, that are stranded on the beach . . . that have no gables and no roofs, that have no floors and no cellars, no up and no down, no front and no back; but that carry in themselves the tensions of the rolling fields, the dead straight lines, the arches and spirals . . . they know the secret of the greatest power in the smallest form, of the noblest line in the fullest mass . . . which are one in inner power, are one in the all-embracing, are one in the all-protecting . . . one in the organic whole!" (H. Th. Wijdeveld).

Is there in fact any area of nature that has a more stimulating and fascinating effect on the designer, the decorator, or indeed anyone who works with color and form than the magical world of shells, which, like thousands of different jewels, are strewn on the beaches of the world's seas or lie buried beneath them?

Is there a greater contrast imaginable in creation than the slimy, shapeless mass of the mollusk and the magnificent house that it builds to protect itself? Are there structures to be found in nature of more radiant beauty, perfect harmony of outward form, or magnificence of color?

The English poet Tennyson, struck by the beauty of shells, wrote:

See what a lovely shell
Small and pure as a pearl
Lying close to my foot,
Frail, but a work divine
Made so fairly well . . .
A miracle of design!

I would urge anyone who is confronted with problems of form, line, and color to collect shells; not to assemble great collections but, in order to understand something of the power of creation, a few varied specimens.

Not only the artist would benefit from this exercise. It would open anyone's eyes to true, genuine beauty, to perfection and clarity, simplicity and richness. It is such a pity that the most magnificent collections of shells lie hidden in dusty boxes and showcases in natural-history museums. They belong in every school and in every home where they can be picked up and handled. In this way people could become reaccustomed to harmony and perfection in color and proportion, in rhythm and melody.

Earlier in this chapter I pointed out snow crystals as an example of one of the working methods of nature, namely, unity in the many.

Every snow crystal is a hexagon, but this basic design is varied a thousandfold. This is also true of shells: we can track down thousands of shells and snail cochlea and examine the secret of their construction; we constantly find new variations of the screw-shaped, ascending spiral. The spiral is one of the most common forms in nature, and we sometimes see shells spinning off into long, pointed shapes; at other times, slowly and thoughtfully forming flat cupolas. The shells illustrated in fig. 9-7 are very beautiful examples of structure and decoration in nature.

Fig. 9-7. (Drawing by Esther Sandmeyer.)

The spiral form is beautiful to behold: not too fast and not too slow, the form rejuvenates itself in ever decreasing circles to the top; in order to refine the form, to accompany it, and above all to strengthen it, the rings perform their own wondrous function, whereby the whole is given a rare perfection. In contrast to the closed top—a definite end—there is the opening of the mouth. It is such a pity that the superb colors forming the crown of this magnificent little palace cannot be shown here. Even a perfect color photograph could scarcely be more than a reflection of the truth, which you must see with your own eyes, feel, and touch: the pink, the mat-white glaze on the inside, and the encrusted old ivory gleaming outside. Everything fits of itself, crystal clear, in thousands of variations and new and wondrous combinations of color and form.

Some shells have a wide, gaping opening through which you can see deep inside; others will not permit such intimacy and have only a narrow opening, well guarded by prickles. Then the interior of the pagodalike little chambers can only be seen from the outside shape, sometimes porcelain blank and unadorned, at other times full of ridges, bumps, prickles, crests, and thorns.

A shell reveals its growth in the tension of the surface lines. A mollusk forms and grows slowly with the growing body, thus creating the beautiful house, artistic, colorful, and clean, which also serves in defence and battle as shelter and protection.

The effects of water can be seen in the forms and colors of shells: the eternally moving, eternally undulating water files the sharp sides and makes the forms fluid and soft. The water contains oxides that, through the animal, give the shell its color and cause it to flow into the magnificent rhythmical patterns that are an endless source of inspiration to the designer who has learned to read the book of nature and whose eyes are open to the colors, structures, forms, lines, rhythms, and tensions.

Endless and tireless, exhilarating and unexpected are the things that nature shows us, both the infinite and vast as well as the small and apparently insignificant and unimportant.

And so the study of a shell, a flower, a crystal always leads us to contemplate the secret of its source, the insoluble question of the origin of all life. I hope that your eyes will be opened and your interest awakened in the real things that stand behind all creative works and that have always been their objective basis.

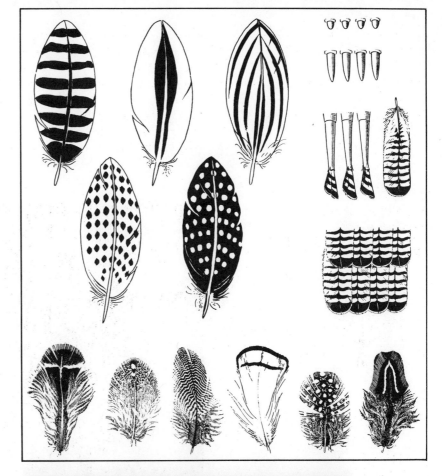

Fig. 9-8. Bird feathers created by the regimented growth of a tissue system based on a ring form. The stripes, burls, and other markings arise in the same way as on shells. Note the rhythmic spatial spreading of the pigments. The right-hand illustration shows a row of feathers in their horny shafts during the first phase of growth. The feathers develop a free, independent, but at the same time symmetrical pattern. The bottom row shows the covert feathers of different pheasants and other birds, forming a closed ornamental pattern. (Drawing by Esther Sandmeyer.)

Fig. 9-9. Zebras: three different species, three different patterns. On the Gray zebra (below) the markings on the hindquarters are similar to those on the forelegs. The Böhm zebra (middle) is dominated by the rearmost diagonal stripe, an evolution which is even more advanced in the Chapman zebra (above), in which a sort of shadow strip appears between the broad stripes. This illustration is an interesting example of ornament in a three-dimensional form. The stripe patterns form a link between other parts of the body, e.g., from hindquarters to belly or from belly to hooves. A completely organic pattern is created, which accentuates eyes, forehead, and the line to the muzzle. (Drawing by Esther Sandmeyer.)

Fig. 9-10. Haeckel has juxtaposed radiolaria (wheeled animalcules, one-celled, with a magnificent lime skeleton) and coral zoophytes.

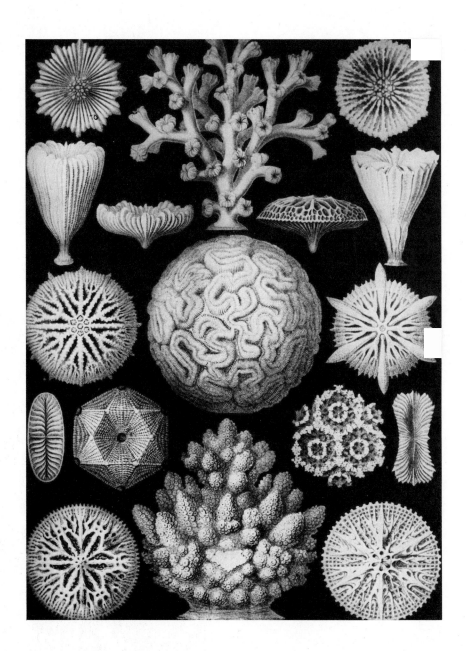

Fig. 9-11. Radiolaria and radiates
(greatly enlarged). These single-celled
creatures live in the sea at all depths, particularly in warmer water. The nucleus,
encapsuled in several layers of proto-
plasm, builds a strangely regular, silice-
ous skeleton, a masterpiece of refined
ornamentation. Sometimes it has a completely geometric shape; sometimes it
has whimsical projections like armored
cars. The microscope reveals thousands
of variations of these miniature construction miracles.

Fig. 9-12. Underside of a five-starred
starfish. The spaces between the projections are closed over. The edge ornamentation and the surface filling have
grown together in a beautiful unison.

Fig. 9-13. Three varieties of conical-shaped shells, each with distinguishing marks. On the largest the ornamentation spiraling toward the point and the roundness of the form create a fine accent. The other two are rather freer in their ornamentation, but they are made interesting by the contrast of larger and smaller shapes.

Fig. 9-14. A miracle of design, down to the last detail. The main form here is again a spiral; the large area is strongly accentuated by the raised surface lines, which run across like ribs. Between the ribs the spaces are filled with a fine ornament, which, together with flecks on the ribs, adds to the spiral accentuation.

Fig. 9-15. The ammonite, some 200 to 300 million years old, proves that even then there were shell-bearing creatures that were already incorporating the spiral principle in their construction. Of the 6,500 varieties of ammonites that have been found imprinted on the chalky soil of middle Europe, only one kind, the nautilus (fig. 9-16), exists today. Enormous ammonites have been discovered with diameters up to three yards.

Fig. 9-16. Cross-section of a nautilus shell with a plastic reproduction. This very ancient species of mollusk has developed a magnificent, geometrically pure spiral to accommodate the animal's need for more living space. In a living nautilus a closed tube runs through curved partitions, through which the animal can increase or decrease the supply of air in order to raise or lower itself.

10. Ornamentation in Folk Art

a.

To understand folk art, we must leave city life and technical progress behind and go back to the land. Until a few decades ago exciting things could be seen in small workshops far from the bustle of the city. Folk art, as I have already said, is primarily rural art, that is, art of the land and the farmer, bound to heaven and earth and creative nature.

The spiritual foundation of folk art was the constant sameness of life, the continuous cycle of the seasons that regulated the course of man's life and work. The interdependence of earth, wind, sun, rain, the blessing of God, the health of man and beast, and the good and evil spirits formed the philosophy of life. Time was regulated by the rising and the setting of the sun and was always the same and constant: it was reflected in the skins of the animals, in the ripening corn, and in busy, creative hands. The wheel of time turned evenly, and between birth and death lay the stations of a endless rhythm of life: work days and feast days, times of joy and times of sorrow. This strong bondage brought with it a strong feeling for tribe, family, and community, living within the same area, on the same land, the same farm, in the same house. Habits, customs, and characteristic symbols were saved and preserved, based on these strong ties, and were made sacrosanct.

This vast bondage of many in one, having the same lifestyle and community, is the characteristic basis of folk unity, the source and foundation of folk art and folk culture. From this ancient unity, based on deep historical roots, came the customs, beliefs, philosophy, dialects, stories, songs, costumes, and handicrafts that we associate with folk art.

Fig. 10-1. (a.) An old Neolithic sign, the lemniscate, made by twisting the circle. Today it is the mathematical sign for infinity. (b.) Other magic knots. (c.) Chest from Graubünden (Switzerland) with sun signs, from the 16th century. (d.) Box with carved sun signs (Switzerland). (e.) Carved decoration on a Basque peasant chest. (f.) Some of the many variations of sun signs.

b.

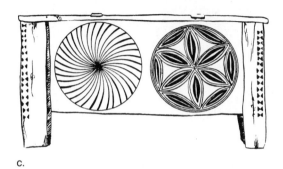
c.

d.

e.

f.

The difference in peoples, in landscape and surroundings, and in materials available account for the differences among mankind as a whole; it is the reason for the variations in color, form, and decoration among different artisans in different places, although all of them were bound together in one great whole—the basic forms, methods of working, and desire to decorate. What these people made for their own use and needs always bore the mark of the strictly functional, but they wanted to do more than that—to make their objects decorative, richer, and more valuable. They decorated with the meaningful signs, symbols, and motifs that had survived, whose deeper meaning and significance was still clearly apparent.

Tools were made according to need and with an eye to certain events: a bridegroom made something for his bride; a bride, for her future household; a farmer, for his business; a mother, for her children; a basketmaker, a potter, a wood turner, or a carpenter, for their customers. It was created where it was used, and thus it gained its value and significance. In a playful fashion and a happy mood all the stimulating, flowery, heart-warming things were created, things which we now collect for the human warmth they arouse in us.

Folk art is conservative but not stiff; it is childish but at the same time self-assured; it imitates yet is original and creative; it is spontaneous but at the same time businesslike and functional; it is full of feeling and deep meaning but sometimes sober, boorish, and rough. It simplifies and stylizes things in a characteristic manner, it absorbs the notions and forms of high art and period styles, extracts the eye-catching and special, yet somehow avoids bad taste.

Folk art is somewhat rough and rustic without losing any value; it exaggerates, consciously or not, even to the point of being grotesque without necessarily wanting to appear original and in so doing creates something totally new, sometimes with surprising results. Its expressive power is great because traditional artistic principles—perspective, anatomy, etc.—are thrown to the wind, even negated entirely: sensitivity and intuitive feeling lead to stimulating, native art. True folk art blossoms beneath the surface even in otherwise less productive eras; in peace and quiet man continues with his work and goes into it just like an artist.

Characteristics of Folk Art

1. Folk art has a symbolic character, although many of the symbols used have lost all but their decorative significance.

2. Fantasy is a striking characteristic—the variations on flowers, tendrils, fruit, and birds, for example, that are adapted in borders, paintings, and etchings are endless.

3. Folk art is honest, open, and unshowy. The reason for this may largely be due to the fact that children's art has survived in folk art.

4. Folk art exhibits an accurate feeling for decoration: difficult technical problems with cutter or paintbrush are solved as if it were child's play. The folk artist, like a child, does not hesitate before such seemingly weighty matters as depictions from the Bible, landscapes, or human and animal figures. He has a pure instinct for arrangement and composition; for end forms, corner accents, headings, and borders. His joy in decoration and his happy pleasure in forms and colors make him unafraid of excess, especially when it is combined with a healthy pride in ostentation: a beautiful room for a rich farmer, a bride's chair, a painted crib, a wedding gown.

5. The use of many strong, unbroken colors characterizes folk art: this is the naive open-mindedness of the natural man. The "sophisticated" art of today is now using strong, unbroken colors. The colors must be powerful, pure, and true; they must radiate and jubilate. The colors are powerfully juxtaposed with one another and clearly separate. It is a joy to see a peasant house interior and the peasant woman in her colorful costume.

6. A kind heart and good humor characterize the art of the people: this is evident in legends and texts on decorated dishes, plates, tiles, cupboards, drinking glasses, and sign boards. Cards and love letters are written in beautiful ornamental letters with lots of curlicues, tongue-in-cheek proverbs, and peasant sayings. A gentle ridicule of life and death, of God and the Holy is not unknown in folk art.

Figs. 10-2 and 10-3. Tapas (cloths) from the Fiji Islands, made with stamps and stencils (of strong leaves) on beaten tree bark. The inside of the paper mulberry bush, a few inches thick, is beaten with heavy wooden paddles into sheets measuring about twenty inches wide. The color of the cloth is creamy white; the ornaments are stenciled in red, brown, and black. Dozens of stencils are used with very little deliberation to make beautiful, strongly geometric ornaments, with a fine feeling for proportion, alternation, and rhythm. Each one exhibits the typical characteristics, but no two tapas are completely alike. The large cloth, below, measures about four by two feet; the smaller one, above, about one by one foot. They are a feast for the eye as a wall decoration and worthy, if simple, representatives of Pacific ornamental art.

Fig. 10-4. Designs have been burned in on calabashes not only in Peru and the rest of South America but also in Africa. In Oceania, Indonesia, and Southeast Asia bamboo is treated in the same way. These calabashes from Southwest Africa, with cut and burnt-in designs, are very decorative. The inside of the dish is decorated with black burnt-in line figures; the outside is partially scraped down to the white wood and burnt on the natural bark. The spoon is a sawed-through calabash and goes with the dish. The round calabash, with a fine, rhythmic burnt-in design, is an attractive holiday souvenir.

Fig. 10-5. Calabash from Peru. The gourd is burnt over a flame to darken it, then the ornament is applied with a fine knife and in a very sensitive manner: three bands of geometric ornamentation: a simple zigzag, a more elaborate one, and a plaited zigzag. The lower surface is decorated with llamas and human figures. The burning and cutting away of parts of the outside layer reveals the natural brown color of the calabash and creates a colorful, ornamental piece of work with its own character.

Fig. 10-6. A Moroccan weaver at her simple loom. These traditional motifs, with their strong geometric forms, free yet orderly rhythm, deliberate restriction to light and dark colors, and fine contrast of vertical and horizontal elements, contain great beauty.

Fig. 10-7. Wrought-iron trivet. The craftsman has made of this simple household article a fine, ornamental piece of work, with spirals and heart shapes. This tool used to be found in every home and farm, and hundreds of them have been preserved in local folklore museums. (Collection of the State Museum for Folk Art, Arnhem.)

Fig. 10-8 (right). Hanover blacksmith's signboard. In this powerful composition he has assembled a collection of tools and implements around the crest of the locksmith. The upright borders are formed by a sort of continuous-wave motif with plantlike elements.

119

Fig. 10-9. Old chest from Westphalia, in which clothing and linen goods were stored. The contrast between the stolid, plain legs, lid, and top borders and the chip carving on the decorated front gives this piece a sturdy, strong character. The dynamic sun wheel also contrasts with the more static sun symbol. Chip carving is a common technique for wood decoration in folk art and rural handicrafts.

Fig. 10-10. Wooden christening font from Sweden, made (turned and cut) from deal wood, circa 1200. The font, about thirty-five inches in diameter, is an example of typically Scandinavian animal figures intertwined with tendrils and leaves. The lower border has a somewhat flat, plaited ornamental design reminiscent of the Roman style. (Photo by Henk van Vliet.)

Fig. 10-11. In the Scandinavian countries folk art, hobbies, and handwork have always played an important role in the life of the people, particularly among farmers in the winter, when work was at a standstill. The availability of many different kinds of wood encouraged their skill. This fine filigree work is made by cutting two pieces of pine, which are squared to one another, with a sharp penknife. The curls form by themselves and stay in this form because of the tension in the wood. Fir can be worked in the same way.

Fig. 10-12. Blueprints from Poland and the Ukraine. These prints were made with wooden printing blocks in which the pattern was cut out. Usually more than one block is necessary for one print. These pieces clearly reveal the technique and the material used.

Fig. 10-13. Polish folk art: scissor cutouts with tree-of-life motif. The Polish art of paper clipping is still very much alive. It is related to and influenced by other techniques (painting, embroidery, etc.) in its single and multiple symmetry.

Fig. 10-14. Motifs from folk art. They are largely borrowed from decorations on unfired ceramic dishes or pots. Wet, white clay is applied on the red background in a linear fashion. The white clay flows from a pointed goose pen stuck in the cork of a bottle or pot containing the clay.

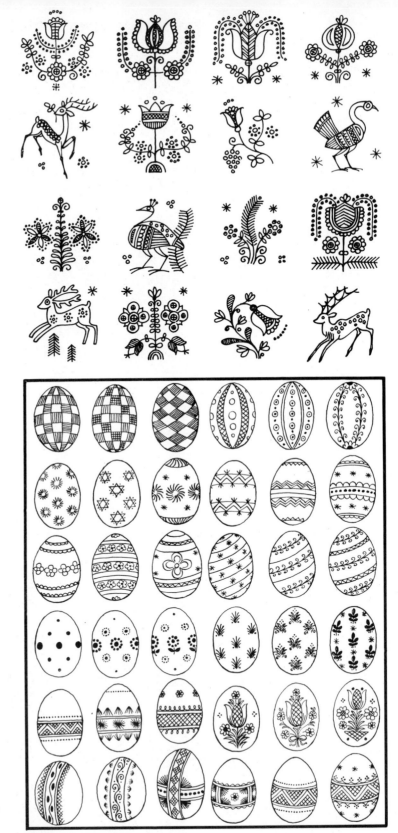

Fig. 10-15. Variations for decorating Easter eggs. These are fine examples of dividing and accenting a particular form in a meaningful way. In South Germany and Eastern Europe (the Balkans) decorating Easter eggs was an important task for housewives and their elder daughters, who were sometimes capable of creating real works of art. The embellishments were applied with a sharp pen in a type of batik or scratching technique.

Figs. 10-16 and 10-17. Prints of Eskimo stone-cutting work. The best-known Eskimo designs are small plastics cut from soapstone, which they have been doing for hundreds of years (see fig. 3-12). They also carved fine geometric designs on bone tools. The Eskimos of Cape Dorset have learned to carve figures of men and animals in stone and then to make prints on paper with paint or ink. These figures illustrate the strong, ornamental talent of these people on the edge of the inhabited world.

11. Ornamentation among Primitive Peoples

Ornament is rhythm made visible. It can be a mark or a sign accenting a certain place. It can be a line to emphasize an ending or divide the area around a shape. It can be a certain motif rhythmically repeated, used in a band or border, or scattered rhythmically over an area. It can be a totally free use of lines, forms, and colors, in which it is difficult to recognize a pattern immediately but which nevertheless exhibits a certain free rhythm and clear balance.

In using forms of nature in ornamentation, be they flowers, waves, plants, butterflies, animals, or human figures, it is not a simple question of filling in certain areas or forms with these motifs. Nor is it a question of artificially stylizing or simplifying them, which usually consists of flattening and exaggerating them. And it is even less a question of manipulating these motifs into "proper" or "usable" shapes. It is, above all, a question of creating rhythm, a totally free rhythm, which in its very movement suggests something of the character, the emotion, and the animation of the artist.

Rhythm, cadence, movement—these are the basic elements of music and dance, and ornamentation is closely related to these arts. It is therefore clear that ornamentation has nothing to do with stylization. The motifs—plants, flowers, animals, the waves of the sea or of a field of corn—have no meaning in themselves if they are not completely subjugated to rhythm and related to the decoration of the surface or object. In order to appreciate music and dance to the fullest, it is essential to understand their meaning, essence, and language. And we also need to learn the language of ornamentation. We need to learn to understand:

1. The many possibilities of the language of line.
2. The essence and the effect of rhythm.
3. The nature and effect of contrast.
4. The meaning of the dynamic.

In every work of art—a painting, a plastic, a building, or an ornament—there is a concealed abstract scheme of construction. This is expressed in the effect of the great axes, horizontal and vertical, which play such an important role in the composition and construction of works of art; in the effect of straight, oblique, and curved lines; and in contrasts of light and dark, stiff and mobile, still and moving, concave and convex. This scheme is like a skeleton: although it is invisible in the body, it maintains life and posture.

124

Fig. 11-1. Mask of the Yoruba tribe, fifteen inches high. For centuries the Yorubas have been masters of bronze casting and wood carving in Nigeria.

Fig. 11-2. Wooden mask, painted black, from the Dan Guere tribe in Africa.

Fig. 11-3. African wood-carvers have created ornamental masterpieces. This lid, in the form of a tattooed human head, shows their work at its finest. It was made by a member of the Bakuba tribe, circa 1900.

This scheme is least concealed in ornamentation: ornamentation wants to be explicit and easily understood—it is not a "free" art. Ornament is subservient and subordinate; it fulfils a role, whether it is on buildings, tapestries, kitchen utensils, or the human body.

It can be totally subordinate and insignificant, or it can emphasize something and focus attention on it; it can increase the worth or meaning of a certain part, it can make it lighter or heavier or higher or lower.

An ornament makes something more valuable and richer if it is well done and not misused by unnecessary elaboration and overemphasis.

A vase that has a good shape and is already enriched by a beautiful glaze does not require further ornament. A space that, through its good proportions and meaningful component parts, pleases the eye does not need additional decoration. Ornamentation in itself is unnecessary and has neither point nor meaning. Only when it is bonded to the article in such a way that it reflects the article's character and enhances it does it gain its value.

But an ornament can also be that little spark of uselessness that adds a certain charm, a little artistic frivolity, a lighthearted touch in the midst of an honest, obvious shape—people need humor now and then in their lives.

Ornament is a language, which is spoken where it is alive and understood. Folk art, that rich, flourishing, and inspiring field, understands ornament in its very naturalness and sometimes childlike naiveté.

The folk artisan, in addition to demands of function and material, could not resist leaving the mark of his own hand and spirit here and there.

True handwork is almost dead. Professional art cultivates it consciously and hence less attractively, but nevertheless with some of the artistic value and meaning that ornamentation used to have. Handwork has been ousted by industrial mass production: ornament—in the usual sense—is not suited to a good industrial product. The function of accenting, defining, dividing has been taken over by trademarks, knobs and handles, inscriptions, chromed piping, and color contrasts.

Ornamentation at its best and finest is still found in the fascinating work of primitive people, people who lived their lives with gods and demons, mystic birds, and protective signs, which they cut and painted on houses and chattels, weapons and vessels; and whose masks, fetishes, and carvings have enormously stimulated and influenced the artists of today.

Fig. 11-4. Melanesian mask (left), almost one yard high, an adornment for the gable of a spirit house; and wooden portrait of a Maori chief from New Zealand (right). The art of these "primitive" peoples is among the most beautiful, expressive, and dynamic ever produced by the hand of man. Ornamentation reached a peak of perfection on shields, boats, and even on common or garden utensils.

Fig. 11-5. Congolese mask; a fine example of large-scale ornamentation in wood.

Figs. 11-6 and 11-7. The Mapaggo women in Basutoland wear broad bands of colored beads around their necks, arms, and legs; moreover, they love to paint their simple white houses regularly with multicolored decorations. In one village they may be mostly geometric (as illustrated here); in another they may prefer architectonic motifs, which make the small houses veritable palaces. The paint they use is not the best quality, and rain and hail sometimes damage the paintings, but when the sun comes out, they cheerfully redo them.

Fig. 11-8. Through the centuries beads have been used as a means of decoration. They are as old as mankind itself: beads of ivory, amber, shells, snails, seeds, teeth, bones, and pebbles remain from prehistoric times. So far, no history of beads has been written. It would indeed be a history of mankind itself, and a very interesting one. These bands of beads come from Africa. The motifs appear to be geometric in character, but in the broader band on the left figure outlines can clearly be seen. The contour lines are in black, against which the colored beads make a good contrast. (Collection of the Mechanische Weberei Pausa company.)

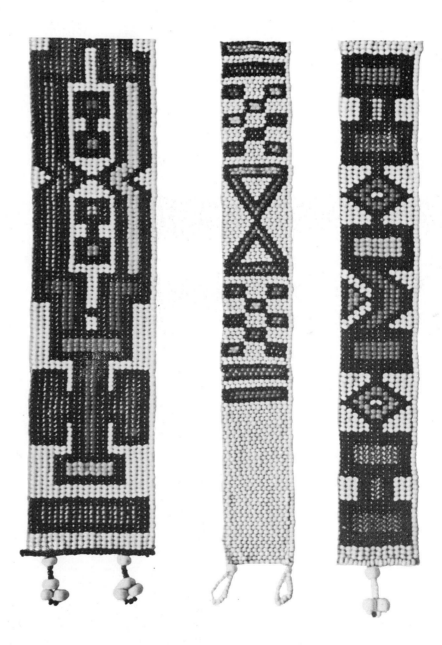

Fig. 11-9. Ritual wooden mask with abstract geometric ornament, from the Teke tribe in the Congo. Masks are ideal objects for decorating: the mask, as a symbol used at feasts and magic rituals, transforms the wearer into another being, sometimes friendly, sometimes frightening. Form and ornament together evoke the desired effect. A very sensitive and lively decoration makes this mask a small masterpiece.

Fig. 11-10. Stamp from the preclassical period of Mexican culture. The central motif is a linear, abstract flower with a cross in the middle; the corners are filled with decorative birds. These stamps, which were made of clay, were used to print cloth and paper. The craftsmen developed a whole range of dyes from plants and minerals. The shapes of the stamps varied: rectangular, round, and triangular. They also made cylindrical seals that were used for ornamental bands and borders.

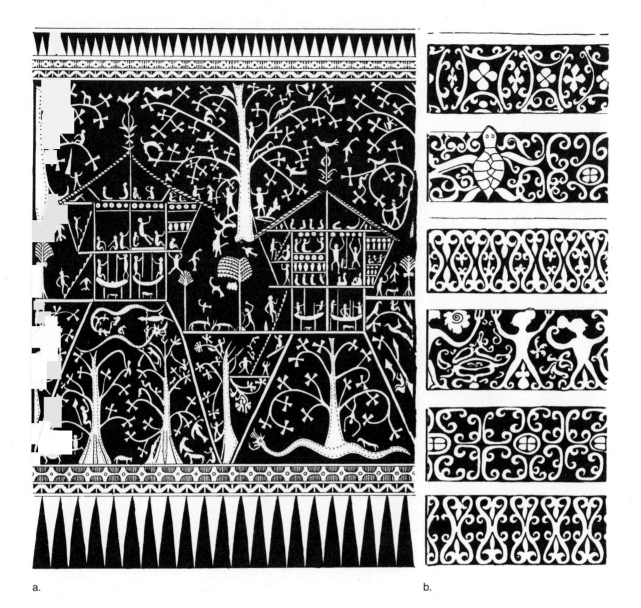

a.

b.

Fig. 11-11. (a.) Bamboo ornament from Borneo. The most beautiful and expressive bamboo ornaments come from the less sophisticated peoples of Indonesia. The lines are burnt in with a piece of coconut shell heated to a glow or engraved with a sharp knife, then the planes are incised. These drawings come from bamboo tubes, which are used in Indonesia to preserve or store things. (b.) Unrolled bamboo ornament from New Guinea. An analysis of these pictures, in spite of the overall unity of effect, shows a rich imagination in depicting the activities of animals and humans. They are masterpieces of ornamental composition, with the fineness of scissor-cutout work. The straight, geometric borders are most effective, even though they tend to keep to traditional forms.

131

Fig. 11-12. Ornaments on bamboo containers from New Guinea. This monumental ornamentation is in keeping with the magnificent, powerful shield designs (see fig. 11-13). These designs exhibit a totally individual character, with an expressive sense of rhythm and a broad application of motif.

Fig. 11-13. Among the most impressive masterpieces of design are the shields from New Guinea, of which a few hundred have been preserved in ethnological museums. The three illustrated here are from the Asmat area. In spite of the increased abstraction of the design, they still have deep symbolic meaning for the native inhabitants. The middle shield is a magnificent, rhythmical depiction of sitting human figures and tree trunks. Using very primitive means, the motifs were cut in relief in the wood and colored black, white, brown, and red. (Collection of the State Museum of Folk Art, Munich; drawings by Alla Seeberg.)

12. Ornamentation in Arts & Crafts

Making things is a primeval need of man. Decorating and ornamentation is no less a need.

Since the beginning man has used whatever materials were at hand to make his life easier and more efficient: from the rough fist wedge came the sharpened ax, a thing of great perfection and beauty; from horn and bone came an array of implements; wood served as a weapon and later as a bow and a drinking bowl.

The hands of man were made to be busy: it is an anthropological phenomenon and an inner compulsion. Consider the achievements of mankind in the course of his history! It would lead us too far astray to investigate this further here. But into work done with his hands he has always poured his heart and soul. Another remarkable phenomenon is that all cultures had this need to refine and decorate what they had made. Handwork and decoration are one, they go hand in hand, they come from one another and merge together. Ornament and handwork are indivisible, and the handmade article is the most fundamental carrier of decoration.

Decoration is so closely bound to handwork that ornamentation created in any other way is scarcely conceivable without being pointless and superfluous. The motivated hand controls the implement, and the handmade article conjures up the decoration by itself: it asks for some meaningful decoration that will add to its value.

Shapes cry out for structure and accentuation; ornamentation gives pleasure in the making and delights the eye of the beholder; it brings life to a plane and tension and rhythm to the interplay of forms. Life itself is decoration and play, rhythm and tension; life and movement are present whenever something is meaningful and valuable.

Good decoration is alive yet unpretentious and subordinate to what it adorns—a vase, a dress, a building. The history of ornament runs parallel with the history of art, for it is art.

When we understand what ornamentation is, we see that hardly any human creation is totally free of it. Think of the oldest things that man has made: it is clear that decoration is inseparable from making the thing itself.

Man is happy and forgets his troubles when he is absorbed in his work. The material to be worked on, through its contrary disposition, makes concentration necessary. Ornamentation is in fact the repetition of a certain motif, and man likes repetition, rhythm, and cadence. The game of material and tool gives peace and gratification, and the creation of ornament is as natural as that of music and dance. Ornament was once something wholly natural, something that flowed from the hands of busy people. When it lost its subordinate, reserved function and freed itself from the object (Renaissance, Baroque, Rococo), it declined. By the end of the nineteenth and the beginning of the twentieth century, fortunately, a feeling for good, responsible composition returned, which revitalized ornament and again firmly tied it to creative handwork.

Precious Metals, Iron, and Bronze

Fig. 12-1. Gilt-silver fibula with garnets from the 7th century A.D. (Collection of the Bavarian National Museum.)

134

Fig. 12-2. Bronze casting from China, Chung period (circa 480 B.C.). This patina-bronze bell is a masterpiece of ornamental art, with the alternation of open and closed shapes, plain and decorated areas, and low and high relief. (Collection of the State Museum, Amsterdam.)

Fig. 12-3. The famous Irish shrine of the Evangelical Book of St. Molaises (died in 563). Decorative plates are set into the bronze frame; the front depicts an Irish wheel cross and the Four Evangelists with gold filigree and inlaid stones.

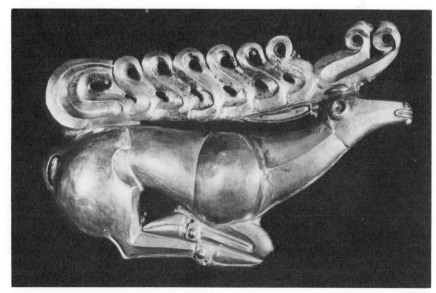

Fig. 12-4. Embossed golden deer, presumed to be a decoration for a round shield, from Scythia. It is eleven inches long and dates from the 7th–6th century B.C. (Collection of the Hermitage Museum, Moscow.)

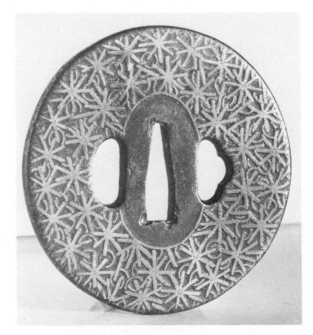

Fig. 12-5. Japanese sword guard *(tsuba)*. In these little masterpieces the Japanese metalworkers achieved the highest standard of craftsmanship and imagination. Thousands of *tsubas* have been made in the course of centuries, mostly by certain families who passed on the trade from father to son. They are all different, mostly made of iron and inlaid (this one, with gold), engraved, and embossed. (Collection of Kalff to Waalre.)

Fig. 12-6. The famous sword of Snartemo from the Viking period of Scandinavia. On both sides of the hilt are panels with animal and plant motifs woven through one another in the so-called animal-figure style. (Collection of the Universitäts Oldsaksammling, Oslo.)

Fig. 12-7. Richly decorated band from an
Evangelical book. The four evangelists
and the heads in the rosettes (center, top
and bottom) are masterpieces of ivory
carving. The other decorations on the
border, the corner rosettes, and the central cross are fine executions of chasing,
filigree, stone cutting, and setting. The
whole is mounted on a wood base. (Collection of the Archbishop Museum,
Utrecht.)

Fig. 12-8. Bishop's staff, richly enameled
in precious metals in Limoges in the 13th
century. (Collection of the State Museum,
Amsterdam.)

Fig. 12-9. Copper and silver bracelet from one of the Dayak tribes of North Sumatra.

Fig. 12-10. Gold ear ornaments with geometric and animal figures in relief from the Chavin culture, Peru (750–250 B.C.)

Fig. 12-11 (below right). Spiraling gold brooch by Alexander Calder, dated 1950. (Photo by Robert Schlingemann.)

Fig. 12-12. (a.) Modern silver rings from the Kilkenny Workshops. (Photo by Con Conner.) (b.) Gold and silver bracelet, designed and executed by Arnoldo Pomodoro. (Photo by Frequin.)

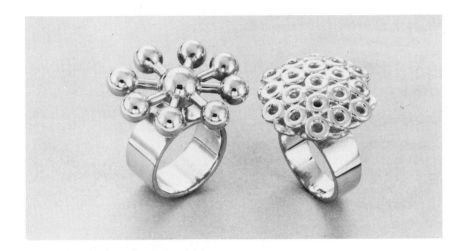

a.

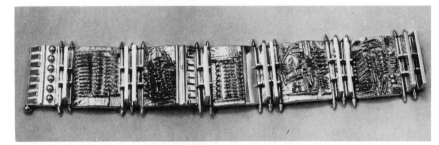

b.

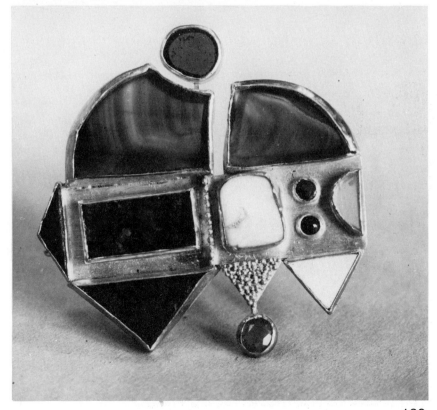

Fig. 12-13. Gold brooch by Herman Jünger, inlaid with cornelian, lapis lazuli, amethyst, and opal. (Photo by Frequin.)

Fig. 12-14. Wrought-iron clock face, designed and executed by Fritz Kühn (1934). The strongly ornamental effect; the clear, direct, and functional form; and the meaningful sign language (sun, moon, heart, sword), together with the filigreelike character of the piece against the coarse stucco wall of a town hall near Berlin, make this a fine example of the adaptation of decorative smithwork to architecture. Until his death in 1967, Kühn cooperated a great deal with architects, often on very extensive projects. His technique, here emphasizing the old smith traditions, was later enriched to include experiments in steel, copper, and aluminum.

Fig. 12-15. Another example of Fritz Kühn's work. This piece has been reproduced here to show how a master craftsman and photographer can create real beauty of form merely by adapting to his material the intrinsic skills of a smith's trade—cleaving, twisting, abutting, hammering, welding, riveting, and pinning.

Fig. 12-16. Ornamental effect obtained with an electric welding machine, by Heiner Krüthoff. This steel relief was made by releasing material in concentric bands around a central square. (Photo by Walter Kneist.)

Fig. 12-17. Ornamental, monumental free plastic by André Volten. It was assembled by welding parts of commercial steel T-beams together. Volten has executed many large plastics for parks, squares, and interiors of important buildings. This structure has an organic construction resembling a tree or bush.

141

Ceramics and Glass

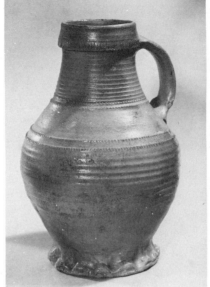

Fig. 12-18. Glazed gray stone jug with handle and pinched foot, from the Rhineland, circa 1400 A.D. The circular markings are well controlled: slightly wider on the body, somewhat finer on the neck; the shoulder is flat in line with the join of the handle; and the collar accentuates the top and provides a sturdy junction for the handle. Several of the circular lines are decorated: the transition from the neck to the shoulder and from the shoulder to the body, as well as the underside of the collar. The crimped foot is handled somewhat more coarsely. (Collection of the Boymans-van Beuningen Museum, Rotterdam.)

Fig. 12-19. Pottery can with pewter lid, eleven inches high, from the Rhineland (circa 1825). It has a gray base with cobalt-blue decoration; the figures are partly stamped on and partly etched by hand with a sharp pen in the leather-hard clay. The decorated field occupies more than half the total surface of the can, with a dominant central motif that is repeated on the sides and flowers filling the rest of the area; blue bands close off the decorated area above and below. This is a popular shape, and there are many local variations in decoration.

Fig. 12-20. Decoration is applied to the pot with a pointed stick after the first drying process in the Kilkenny Workshops.

142

Fig. 12-21. Vase designed by Lies Cousijn and fabricated by the De Porceleyne Fles studio. A black surface is applied to the white clay, on which the ornament is scratched: it is a free-form decoration that covers the body of the vase like a cobweb. The design is mainly vertical, with a sensitive contrast of horizontal circular lines and circles strewn over the surface.

Fig. 12-22. Dish by Dirk Hubers. It has a sketchlike ornament in black on a light-gray background.

Fig. 12-23. Bowl by Bruno Bruni. The decoration consists of abstract stripes and flecks, which were scratched on a glazed surface. (Collection of the Royal Academy of Art's-Hertogenbosch; photo by Louis van Beurden.)

Fig. 12-24. Earthenware jug by Picasso (1948), decorated with centaurs.

Fig. 12-25. Earthenware bottle with scaled belly, designed and executed by Sonja Landweer. This distinctive and clearly defined shape—a flowing transition from collar, neck, and shoulder into the forceful, domineering body with profiled foot—acquired its vitality, richness, and refinement through a pattern of vertical rows around the body. Each of these rows was made by pressing a small stick point upwards into the clay and was further emphasized by the glaze finish.

Fig. 12-26. Beaker with burls, made in Northern France, circa 1400. Even in olden times glass was decorated in many ways. Here, the molten-glass surface was infused with liquid glass in the shape of points, burls, droplets, and lines. The contrast between the plain upper rim and the greenish burled body is pleasant to the eye. (Collection of the Simon van Gijn Museum, Dordrecht; photo by Rijks Oud-heidkundig Bureau.)

Fig. 12-27. Crystal service, made by the Leerdam glass factory from a design by Copier, 1965. A strong ornamental effect is obtained by repeating the ball motif in different sizes and singly or in groups.

Fig. 12-28. Crystal vase, designed by Max Verboeket. The ornament is made of stripes and lines of colored glass, which acquired this whimsical form in the blowing process.

145

Weaving, Wood, and Ivory

Fig. 12-29. Simple, round straw mat with a reinforced border. The horizontal and vertical weaving, used to create a beautiful, ornamental diamond pattern, is clearly discernible.

Fig. 12-30 (above right). What Japanese basket weavers can do with split bamboo borders on the unbelievable: this sample gives only a mild taste of their work, but the lively contrast between the concentrically linked circles and the finely woven central ornament is worth noting.

Fig. 12-31. Ornamental basket of pulp cane, fourteen inches in diameter. Form and ornament are closely allied and in fact develop from the weaving technique: the sturdy base in the center opens into a finer, interlacing weave, which is surrounded by a sturdy outer edge with a woven strip in between to strengthen the open latticework. The outside rim of larger and smaller semicircles develops from the broad band and creates a beautiful, organic border accent. Such a basket, simple though it may be, is an almost perfect piece of handwork—logical, organic, beautiful.

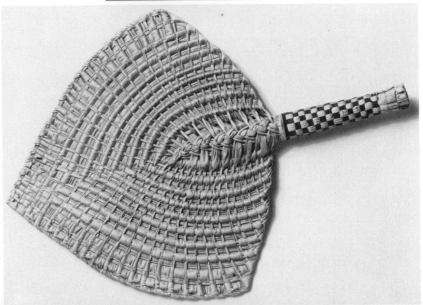

Fig. 12-32 (opposite, bottom). African and Pacific craftsmen make these fans to dispel heat and flies. They are perfect in form, structure, and joins; perfect in technique; and perfectly serving their purpose. From the method of working and the material itself an organic entity of the highest order is created, in which the visible construction itself adds great ornamental value. Apart from the chessboard design on the handle, no extra decoration has been added. (Photo by Frans Grummer.)

Fig. 12-33. Small basket (four inches in diameter) from Bangkok. The base is split bamboo.

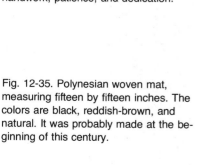

Fig. 12-34. African pointed baskets. The taller of the baskets, seventeen inches high, is made of grass fibers wrapped around a sturdy core with a very fine ornament of dyed grasses. The small one is only four inches high, but its precision of structure makes it a masterpiece of handwork, patience, and dedication.

Fig. 12-35. Polynesian woven mat, measuring fifteen by fifteen inches. The colors are black, reddish-brown, and natural. It was probably made at the beginning of this century.

147

Fig. 12-36. Chinese ball. This master-piece of Eastern craftsmanship consists of fourteen loose balls, which sit within one another. Each ball is successively cut loose through the holes of the surrounding ball from one massive piece of ivory, an undertaking that lasts for years. Each ball has a pierced ornament with a different motif: the inner balls have geometric designs; the outer ball, figure and plant motifs. What the Chinese craftsmen have achieved in this medium borders on the unbelievable.

Fig. 12-37. Until the present day and in spite of its enormous industrial explosion, handwork has always been an important element in Japanese life. This mat is an example of simple ingenuity and feeling for design, and it looks delightful on the table. Thick and thin bamboo stalks are glued into a bundle and then sawed into thin layers.

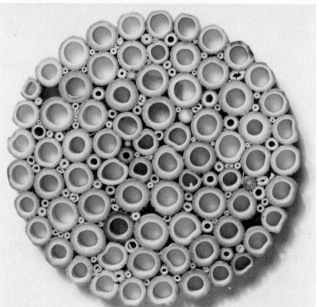

Fig. 12-38. Rosewood dish, turned by Jochen Winde, six inches in diameter at rim. The hyperbolic form is nicely divided and accentuated by the five broader bands and the smooth base and top rims. The finer lines between these bands contribute not only a fine contrast but also a lively structure to the intervening areas.

Fig. 12-39. Pitch-pine dish, turned by Jochen Winde, eight inches in diameter. Nature has provided its own design through the hands of the craftsman who knew how to reveal it in a particular shape.

Textile Arts

Fig. 12-40. Decorative stitching on a tunic from the Christian graveyard in Egypt; the motifs themselves are borrowed from Greek mythology. The figures are made of dyed-black wool, and the tunic is linen. Thousands of these pieces have been found, some with several colors. This one dates from the 4th–5th century A.D. (Collection of the State Museum of Antiquities, Leiden.)

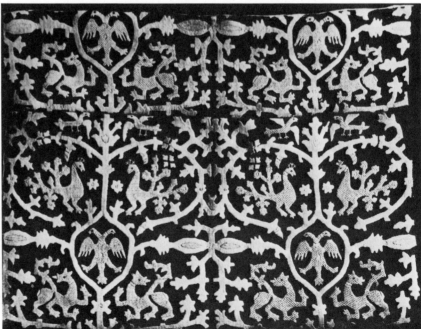

Fig. 12-41. Russian tapestry from the 16th century. (Collection of the Historisch Museum, Moscow.)

Figs. 12-42 and 12-43. Batikwork; the center panel of a screen by Chris Lebeau and a silk wrap by Chris Lannooy, respectively.

Fig. 12-44. Table linen designed by Chris Lebeau in 1930.

Fig. 12-45. *Klavier,* a woven wall hanging by Maria Laszkiewitz. It was made in 1963 and measures about twelve by nine feet. This attractive hanging is strongly ornamental in construction, with a vertical emphasis, horizontal pianolike accents, and fine structural and tonal contrasts.

Fig. 12-46. Detail of *Spain,* a wall hanging by Thea Gregoor (1963). It is an appliquéd patchwork collage, measuring about six by three feet. The magnificent, richly contrasting color distribution and the sensitive ornamentation combine into a harmonious whole and make this piece a fine example of ornamental textiles. (Collection of the Stedelijk Museum, Amsterdam.)

Fig. 12-47. *Organ,* another woven wall hanging by Maria Laszkiewitz (measuring about six by five feet). Two large diamond shapes dominate the middle field in an otherwise geometrically divided tapestry. The deep pile softens the lines and edges and contributes its own character to this hand-knotted piece. (Photo by Stedelijk van Abbemuseum.)

Fig. 12-48. Detail from *Sunrise,* a wall hanging by Krystyna Wojtyna-Drouet (1972). It measures about seven by ten feet. (Photo by Bert van Goethem.)

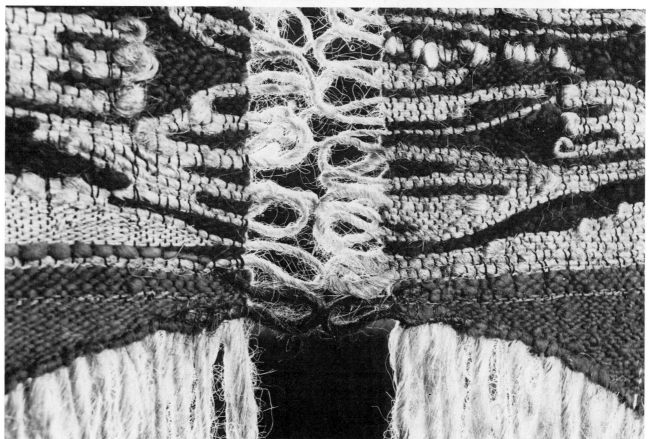

Fig. 12-49. *Lovely weaves,* a series of tableaux by Ria van Eyk, made by plaiting strips of vinyl. They are enlargements of fundamental base forms in weaving called bindings. Each tableau contains an equal quantity of black and white arranged differently. The plaiting is regular, and the width of each strip is the same, creating a series of eight related tableaux based on squares.

Fig. 12-50. Some more experimental tapestries by Ria van Eyk, again constructed from simple bindings. Horizontal and vertical bindings create static lines, which blend into more dynamic herringbone diagonals and a diamond pattern.

Fig. 12-51. Another experimental tapestry by Ria van Eyk. Strips of silver vinyl were used to make this herringbone design.

154

Fig. 12-52. Design by Adolf Felger, based on African motifs. The typical African character has been preserved in the designs, which, through their power and simplicity, suit the modern interior very well. (Collection of the Mechanische Weberei Pausa company.)

Fig. 12-53. *Mariella,* curtain material designed by the Ploeg design team. It was executed in various color schemes.

Fig. 12-54 (below right). *Damon,* curtain material designed by Jeanne Schaap, also executed in various color schemes.

Fig. 12-55. *Spanish Lace,* a design for mechanically woven or knitted lace, by Jack Lenor Larsen. This simple but very sensitively composed geometric interplay of thicker and thinner lines with accentuated knot points is based on a logical division of the square and the diamond.

Fig. 12-56 (above right). Detail of the lacework borders in a large altar cloth designed and executed by Hanna von Allmen.

Fig. 12-57. (a.) *Ise Katagami,* fabric with a flower motif, by Yoshimatsu Nambu. The design is printed on the fabric with a hand-cut paper stencil. The stencils are cut in the traditional manner and used for printing kimono materials and other decorative fabrics and paper. They are cut from strong, handmade paper and pasted on top of one another for strength: several layers are cut at one time. Some designs contain 900 openings on a surface area of one inch square. The advent of machine-made stencils and machine printing has not disturbed the masters of this craft, for they well know that no machine will ever be able to match the unbelievable skill of their hands nor their limitless fantasy. (b.) Fish motif and geometric theme by an unknown craftsman.

a.

b.

13. Ornamentation in Industrial Products

The search for new possibilities in our technology must be based on a just diagnosis of the subject itself, which was not provided by the virulent attacks of Loos or Morris.

Ornamentation, decoration, and embellishment require our renewed attention today, whether we like it or not. A new trend towards kitsch and romanticism is clearly discernible, even in composition. This deterioration cannot be avoided by passing judgment on the buying public from the lofty heights of our ivory towers: "Your wishes are the expression of a decadent 'chocolate-box' taste, and it doesn't affect me!"

I do not believe that the decors created by our gifted designers should be written off and set aside as a cultural phenomenon in an arts-and-crafts museum: the desire to decorate and add luster cannot be arbitrarily dismissed from composition today.

Generally speaking, decoration is considered acceptable for fabric, printing, and wallpaper. Only for a limited number of people has the totally white service, for example, become a sign of better living and a status symbol: the vast majority of the buying market wants some decoration and color on earthenware and porcelain. Self-respecting businesses have gone to great lengths to find acceptable solutions, with considerable success.

We are discussing here mechanized decorations, which are obviously not painted on but drawn, duplicated, and applied by modern technological means. This is the only sort of solution, in my opinion, that will satisfy the need to enrich the form yet remain consistent with the spirit of our times.

There is another circumstance in the case of porcelain that supports decoration. A fairly large quantity of porcelain is flawed after its first firing in the oven—which is why it was and still is customary to cover these small mistakes with a decoration in order to distract the eye.

In recent years decoration of glass has increased considerably, particularly glass used in lighting installations. The same is true of cutlery and silverware. These products, which are handed down from generation to generation, are only minimally subject to the whims of fashion. Since their gleam and cool beauty easily attract the eye, they require scarcely any decoration. From the point of view of usage, e.g., in order to get a better grip, a decoration is not justifiable. What the market desires is the deciding factor in favor of decoration. Acceptable solutions for cutlery and silverware are more difficult than for porcelain and glass.

In trying to formulate general guidelines for relevant decoration in this day and age, it must be remembered that only the hand and creative spirit of a gifted designer can bring any decoration to life. The decoration must emerge in an organic way and be related to the material on which it is being used. A contemporary decor is not good if it does not clearly reveal the technique of its creation.

Contemporary reproduction techniques can do everything; we must use this power carefully, with wisdom and restraint. A hand-painted flower decoration was appropriate to the eighteenth-century style, but it is tasteless to reproduce it with a glued-on-picture, however successfully we can do it.

Decor must remain modest and subservient: it should not attract too much attention or be anything more than a fine, meaningful accompaniment to the shape.

We must continue to cultivate the clean, pure, clear, undecorated form and at the same time search for the right forms of decoration, which can be regarded as an essential by-product of the development of this primeval human phenomenon.

The "prophets" of pure form eschew all decoration, with the exception of curtain and furniture fabrics. Consumers from certain intellectual and artistic milieus until quite recently preferred the undecorated form. Nowadays they lean toward "modern" forms and want to see them elevated by a discreet and appropriate decor.

Most consumers give little thought to good form. They have not yet learned to value things on their own merits: they value the outward glitter of richness and luxury. Hence, in our stores we see two distinct worlds: on the one hand careful attention to form, quality, color, and decor, in both the manufacture and the sale; and on the other no attention to form and quality, merely a superficial beauty and tinsel. Between the two, naturally, there are intermediate stages in the manufacturers and their products. In order to achieve a gradual improvement, designers must continue to pay attention to good composition and no less to good decoration. Wholesalers, storekeepers, department heads, and sales personnel must be well trained, and young people must be taught, beginning in the elementary schools, what better life and living mean in our times: they must learn to understand the meaning of good composition, and they must have the opportunity to form their own judgments. Then the problem of ornamentation and decoration would be solved.

Fig. 13-1. The famous Landi chair, designed by Corray and Blattmann in 1938. The stackable chair is made of aluminum and therefore very light. The holes in the back and seat form a natural and organic ornament and reduce the weight.

Fig. 13-2. Tubular steel chair designed by Mart Stam in 1928 and produced by Thonet. This chair can be reckoned among the best industrial products in Europe. The woven seat and back contrast well with the steel frame and at the same time contribute ornamental richness.

Fig. 13-3. The majority of the public still tends to buy crockery decorated with flowers or other curlicues. Lack of good taste or enlightened education makes many people fail to recognize the simplicity of a good product, and they grab for things that, through exaggeration or decoration, appear to be more than they are. A good design needs no—or very little—decoration. A few porcelain factories, such as Mosa, whose service in white and midnight blue designed by Heinrich Löffelhardt is illustrated here, have dedicated themselves to the task of compromising between the desire for decoration and plain, undecorated tableware. This two-tone coffee service, with fluting supporting the vertical lines, may well serve as a successful attempt.

Fig. 13-4. Cassette tape recorder, designed and manufactured by Philips. Here again, there is no conscious ornamentation, but rather an interplay of functional elements that creates an ornamental effect. The choice of materials and colors naturally plays a part.

Fig. 13-5. Pocket tape recorder, designed by Philips. Placing the technical elements on the surface and etching into the matrix form the organic ornamentation on this product.

Fig. 13-6. *Modern Heraldry*, a photomontage of ornamental decorations and lamps from postwar American automobiles. They are for the most part products of the fatal desire for styling and have no relation whatsoever to organic ornament.

14. Ornamentation in Architecture

Ornament literally means "decoration" or "embellishment." It is not strange, therefore, that when we examine a building such as a temple, cathedral, or pagoda—not infrequently the most beautiful jewel in a city—we regard the ornamentation as the most important part. Even a city itself can act as a jewel in the landscape, as an ornament in the broadest and highest sense.

We are touching on border territories here: ornamental architecture and architectural ornament merge into each other. In architecture we must in fact classify as ornament whatever is over and above the strictly functional and necessary. The row of columns surrounding the actual sanctuary of a Greek temple falls into this category and forms in fact the most beautiful monumental ornament that we can conceive of.

And yet we regard these columns as belonging to architecture and not to ornament. This is also true of profiles and cornices, which constructively speaking are not strictly essential. On the other hand we speak of ornamented cornices, surfaces, and columns and thereby clearly indicate the secondary, accompanying role of the ornament in architecture. Consequently, we realize that ornament in architecture can only be fairly judged in conjunction with the whole edifice.

Whenever an ornament obtrudes, demands too much attention, and wants to play an independent role, our artistic sensitivity—our sensitivity to balance and order—is disturbed. An ornament taken out of the context of its surroundings and executed on another scale or in another medium quickly becomes a disfiguration.

A formula for the use of ornament in architecture must be based on the close connection of all the elements that play a role, e.g., the goal and function of the construction and the meaning of contrast, rhythm, proportion, relative size, direction, unity, and use of materials. The need for simplicity and reserve will often result in wholly or partially eschewing all decoration.

A meaningful affinity to nature and the organic will prevent the artist from straying. A pure feeling for the materials and their structural and functional possibilities is just as indispensable to meaningful ornamentation.

Architecture through the centuries has displayed all the different varieties of ornament: Stonehenge and the monuments in Brittany; the edifices in Babylon, Assyria, and Egypt; Greek, Etruscan, and Roman work; the miracles of Chinese and Japanese ornamental architecture; the temples in India, Cambodia, Bangkok, and Java. Ornamental art was used with particular richness in countries where Islam had a firm hold—Persia, the Middle East, North Africa, and Spain (the Alhambra, for example).

Closer to us are the medieval cathedrals, in which the ornamental art of the stone masons rivaled that of the glaziers, mosaic makers, and tapestry weavers. Of a totally different structure and character is the ornamentation of the religious temple cities of the Toltecs, Mayas, Aztecs, and Incas in Central and South America.

The decline of true ornamental art began in the Renaissance with exaggerated and nonsubordinate decoration and reached its nadir in the nineteenth century, when architecture lost its true sources of inspiration and sank into a weak imitation of classical and medieval styles.

Around the turn of the century a healthy rejuvenation of building and decorative art began in Europe. Van Doesburg and Mondrian, among others, made an important contribution to ennobling and purifying the plastic and related arts. There was a natural reaction to the pure and doctrinaire functionalism, in which the art of ornamentation scarcely had a chance, and nowadays ornamentation has once more established an important place for itself in architecture.

Hundreds of works of art executed in every conceivable medium—bronze, iron, stone, plastics, mosaics, leaded glass, concrete, murals, tapestries, ceramics, wood—decorate our modern buildings and their surroundings. Ornamentation and related arts are used to a great extent in architecture today.

Fig. 14-1. (a.) Corinthian capital from Tholos, circa 340 B.C. (b.) Ionic capital from the Propylaean Temple at the Acropolis in Athens, circa 475 B.C.

a.

b.

a.

Fig. 14-2. (a.) Doric capital from the
Aphaia Temple at Aegina, circa 500 B.C.
(b.) Romanesque ornament, Saint Wal-
derich Church, Murrhardt, early 13th century.

Fig. 14-3. Figures on the west column
portal of the Chartres Cathedral (circa
1140). These four figures are effective
not only because of their vertical
straightness and the refined treatment of
the folds, which emphasizes the vertical
lines, but also because they are one of
the most characteristic applications of
ornament in architecture. The rich ornamentation between the figures adds
yet another special element of contrast.

Fig. 14-4. Large rose window on the west façade of the Strasbourg Cathedral (circa 1300). The ornamental filling of this large square with an enormous circle, with its finely balanced divisions and proportions and its rich effect (particularly beautiful fillings of the corners), makes this one of the high points of ornamentation in architecture.

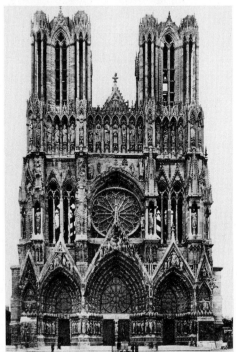

Fig. 14-5. The early Gothic west façade of Rheims Cathedral (13th century).

Fig. 14-6. The Koran prohibits in principle the depiction of men and animals in painting or carving. Islamic architecture has consequently developed geometric ornamentation to a very fine art. This is true of the architecture itself as well as the rich decoration. (a.) Examples of stalactite ornamentation, which is used in many variations. (b.) Carved and turned wooden panel fillings.

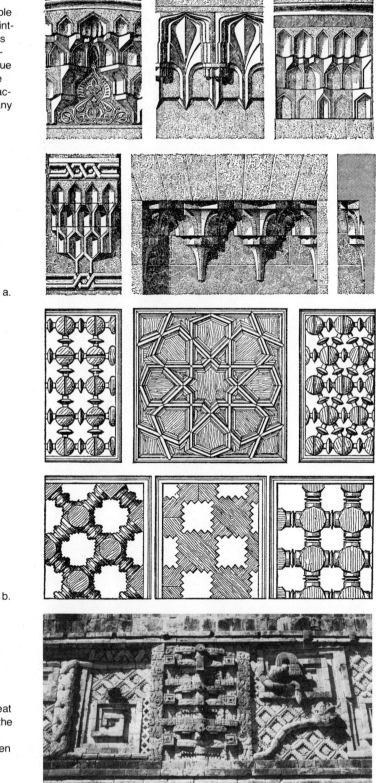

a.

b.

Fig. 14-7. Geometric decorations of great ingenuity and diversity fill the walls of the Maya temples of Uxmal in Yucatan, Mexico. Next to them and often between them are human and animal figures (snakes, turtles, jaguars, eagles) and masks.

165

Fig. 14-8. A totally different kind of ornament in architecture, used in railings, entrances, lighting fixtures, balcony decorations, gratings, and trelliswork, has been in existence for centuries. There are magnificent examples, mostly in wrought iron, in South Germany, Switzerland, Italy, Spain, and Portugal. This figure shows an example of the typical English-Irish Georgian style, which is located at Steffen's Queen in Dublin. (Photo by Ria van Eijck.)

Fig. 14-9. Detail of the Willem II cigar factory at Valkenswaard (Architektenburo Bogers en Van der Hoogen, architect). This construction exhibits a good rhythmic division of façades, especially the large steel skeleton.

Fig. 14-10. Bronze sculpture by Arthur Sproncken. It is placed against a background of natural stone, and there is a light inside so that it appears to stand free from the wall in the evening.

Fig. 14-11. Large ornamental object by Thea Gregoor, executed in painted jute and foam rubber.

Fig. 14-12. These water reservoirs are particularly decorative when illuminated at night.

15. Ornamental Trends in the Free Arts

In spite of the imprecations of Loos and the purists of the new functionalism, a demand for ornamentation has evolved in all directions.

Loos turned against the pointless, exaggerated, overpowering ornamentation of his time, but he threw the baby out with the bath water. The advent of van de Velde and the Jugendstil gave ornamentation new energy, even though it was a climbing weed that overgrew everything.

Not until the work of Hoelzel, Kandinsky, Klee, Matisse, Herbin, Picasso, Baumeister, Mondrian, and van Doesburg, as well as folk and primitive art, became influential did new and healthy ornamental trends reemerge. None of these artists wanted their work to be classified as ornamental, in spite of the fact that it expressed strong ornamental tendencies. Klee, for example, never mentions ornament in his books. The last works of Mondrian, e.g., *Victory Boogie-Woogie,* are without doubt strongly ornamental, and van Doesburg's *Kaartspeler* is built up in the same way, although the result is less emphatic.

Baumeister, Picasso, and particularly Matisse use many ornamental elements, although they are incorporated not as decoration but as elements in composition. A much clearer and more direct use of ornamental elements is evident in the work of younger, mostly living artists: Vasarely, Capogrossi, Hundertwasser, Bubenik, Götz, Stella, Noland, Davis, Dubuffet, Manessier, Miró, Alan Davie, Tucker, Tilson, Riley, Pomodoro, Bay, Hans Arp, Max Bill, and many others.

This new ornamentalism is something other than ornamentation, which always had a subservient and applied function. Traditional ornamentation accompanied styles and could, by close association with an object or building, take its place among the applied arts.

The new ornamentation in free art is an independent art form. Through strong but often restrained composition it achieves the power and expressiveness that has always fascinated man. Sometimes, however, it is merely empty ornamentation, for it does not fulfil its subservient role.

Apart from ornamental elements art in this century has taken up many structural aspects. Often the border between ornament and structure is very vague. A discussion of ornamentation as art rather than decoration seems to be fruitless. As Hoelzel said, "It is not the richness of the form itself that is harmful but the rich form in the wrong place."

Paul Klee has been able to bypass every form of decoration by means of almost imperceptible deviations from regularity.

Everything in the last analysis depends on the quality of the work itself: refinement, sensitivity, ingenuity; feeling for form, size, and color. The magic of the creative spirit and not the stiffness of a measured-out, dry decoration is true ornamentation.

The new ornamental art is: nonperspectival, antiillusionistic, and dimensional: it ties ratio to feeling and creativity and connects science with art and the irrational. As Max Bense writes: "Ornaments of all times are macroaesthetic forms of symmetry, which strive in our time for self-autonomous aesthetic realization."

Fig. 15-1. *Composition IX* by Theo van Doesburg. This panel was painted in 1917 by a continuous process of abstraction toward horizontal planes and lines.

Fig. 15-2. *Composition with blue* by Piet Mondrian. (Collection of the Gemeentemuseum, The Hague.)

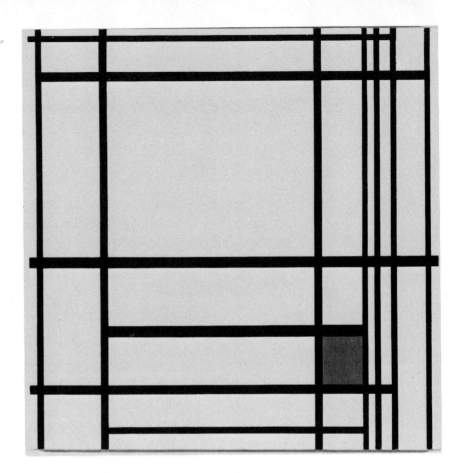

Fig. 15-3. *Keichter Verfall* by Paul Klee (1927). In his own work and in lessons to his students, Klee combined the ornamental and the geometric in a constantly fascinating and fantastic way.

Fig. 15-4 (below right). The work of Henri Matisse has always had a strongly ornamental character. Clothing, flowered wallpaper, wall hangings, plants, and fish were always part of his compositions and carriers of his strong colors. As he grew older and painting became more difficult for him, he made interesting collages with scissors and colored paper, such as the *Jazz* series, of which the illustration here is a black-and-white example. He made hundreds of variations on this theme and also adapted it for the chasubles, windows, and walls of the little chapel at Vence, which he completely designed and decorated.

Fig. 15-5. Richard P. Lohse, a Swiss artist, has devoted a large part of his life to paintings whose forms and colors are created on the basis of systems.

Fig. 15-6. Frank Stella is reckoned among the "postpainterly abstractionists" because of the spatial and linear character of his work. From 1958 to 1966 he used simple, geometric, and monochrome patterns, often in aluminum. The illustration shown here is a graphic from this period.

Index